NEUTRALITY
A Policy for Britain

NEUTRALITY
A Policy for Britain

Peter Johnson

Temple Smith · London

First published in Great Britain in 1985
by Maurice Temple Smith Ltd
Jubilee House, Chapel Road
Hounslow, Middlesex, TW3 1TX

Johnson, Peter
Neutrality.
1. Neutrality
I. Title
327   JX5361

ISBN 0-85117-255-5

Typeset by Margaret Spooner Typesetting, Dorchester, Dorset.
Printed in Great Britain by The Camelot Press, Southampton.

CONTENTS

1   Foreign Policy   1

2   The Super-powers: (1) The Soviet Union   10

3   The Super-powers: (2) The United States   23

4   The Super-powers in the World   28

5   What Kind of War?   37

6   British Defence: The Status Quo   50

7   Aspects of Neutrality   59

8   British Neutrality and Foreign Policy   77

9   British Neutrality and Defence   91

10   British Neutrality and the World   111

11   British Neutrality and the British   128

1. *Foreign Policy*

If you advertised a meeting in your local Town Hall as being about NUCLEAR WEAPONS TODAY or BAN THE BOMB! you might easily get a full house. People would encourage or argue with the speakers. The issues are live and the man and woman next door have views. If, however, you said that the meeting was to be about FOREIGN POLICY you might fill the back row. Yet everyone is interested in the idea of peace and it is the foreign policies of nations which control the roads to peace or war.

In most democracies foreign policy is partly segregated from the frictions and clashes of political faction. Practical considerations limit the participation of the electorate, and even of parliamentary representatives, in day-to-day decisions, which are left to professionals and experts. Nevertheless the general thrust of foreign policy affects everyone and is far too vital a matter to be ignored by the man and woman in the street. A director of the Royal Institute of International Affairs has written (*The Times*, May 1981), that 'foreign policy is slowly being democratised'. He added that this is 'certainly enough to make Lord Curzon spin in his grave'. Well, let Lord Curzon spin. The more widely great issues are discussed, the more likely it is that right decisions will be made. Closed doors breed closed minds.

Arguably the most important and certainly the most spectacular aspect of foreign policy is that of national security, which includes the problems of national defence. By decisions in this field nations get themselves into wars and, sometimes, avoid or prevent them. Security, as well as many other components of foreign policy, is based on what is called in the jargon an 'orientation', which fixes and describes a nation's general attitude and commitments to the rest of the world. The place, and to a great extent the behaviour, of that nation on the international scene depends largely on the orientation it maintains.

Orientation is influenced, sometimes dictated, by physical, geographical, industrial, financial, political, military, ideological, moral and religious characteristics and circumstances. One or more of these may be vital or decisive, so that a nation's orientation can be imposed by factors beyond the control of its government or people. Changes of circumstances may suggest or dictate a change of orientation, although outworn orientations can and do survive through lethargy, indifference or vested interest.

Ignoring for the moment the division between rich and poor nations, the international environment has tended to polarise about the hostility between Russia and the United States, and the orientations of many other nations relate, in part at least, to their attitudes towards this military and ideological rivalry which dominates our planet. An orientation towards the super-powers does not necessarily inhibit other tendencies or groupings, but it will usually have an effect on such relationships. It is convenient to classify the orientations available under three headings, Isolation, Non-alignment and Alliance.

Isolation consists of the attempt to reduce contacts and transactions with other states to the minimum. As a policy it is scarcely available nowadays. Only states with a high degree of self-sufficiency and a low requirement for external trade can adopt it.

Such states as China, Mongolia, Japan, Turkestan, Ethiopia, and Siam struggled to maintain their isolation until well into the nineteenth century, but all, however reluctantly, eventually abandoned the stance. In this century China and Burma have experimented with isolation, but both have now renewed contacts and increased trade with the outside world.

The expresion 'Splendid Isolation' was often used to describe the British orientation in the nineteenth century and the word 'Isolationism' has been used for the United States' attitude to the League of Nations between the wars. Neither of these policies was isolation in the technical sense because both countries were intensely occupied in close contacts with other countries in every part of the world.

Communist nations try to isolate their peoples from all outside influence but, since their governments take a full part in international affairs, they cannot be described as isolationist.

Non-alignment essentially means that a state will not commit itself or its resources to the military support of another state or power bloc, that it will not voluntarily take part in war with or between other states and that it proposes to pursue a policy of neutrality in any war. The stance entails single-handed responsibility for the security and defence of national territory and interests, except in so far as faith can be reposed in the terms of the Charter of the United Nations or, in some cases, in specific guarantees by outside powers. Under the heading of non-alignment there is sometimes confusion between the terms 'neutrality', 'neutralisation' and 'neutralism'. The technical differences are not unimportant but, for the time being, we shall take it that they are all aspects of the same basic concept of non-alignment.

The third orientation available is that of *Alliance* or Coalition. Combinations between political units, often but not always primarily for military purposes, have been practised since the earliest times. Groupings are recorded within the early Chinese state system, between the city-states of Greece and Italy, among the Indian tribes of North America and throughout the history of the quarrelsome nation-states of Europe.

Alliances may derive from states believing that their own resources are inadequate to achieve objectives which they particularly desire or for the joint defence of interests or territories they see as threatened. Greater aggressive power or extra defensive capability can be acquired by an alliance, but the stance also increases the risk of involuntary involvement in the quarrels or commitments of a partner. Nearly all alliances are 'defensive' in the eyes, and certainly in the published declarations, of their members.

An alliance is often used by a greater power as an excuse to interfere in or control the affairs of a lesser state. Installing, supporting or perpetuating a regime convenient or subservient to the patron and influencing the pattern of trade, foreign relations or defence are parts of the normal currency of alliance. Not all alliances succeed in serving the purposes for which they were constructed and unwilling partners tend to desert under strain. It is a historical cliché that coalitions formed to fight a war against a specific enemy have seldom survived for long the coming of peace.

A nation's foreign policy should be based on the main goals

or aims which it hopes to achieve on behalf of its people. The choice of a foreign policy orientation should, therefore, depend on those goals.

A nation's aims or goals, towards which its foreign policy contributes, can be divided into three categories.

First are those which are basic, permanent and central to the life and well-being of the country. Examples are national security and independence, the preservation of frontiers, the safety of supplies of food and essential materials and the safeguarding of national integrity, ideology or religion. The security, stability or co-operation of neighbours or strategic areas beyond national frontiers may be regarded as 'vital' interests. In the past Britain regarded the control of the seas as vital for her imperial communications, the recovery of the lost provinces of Alsace and Lorraine was a 'core' objective for France after the Franco-Prussian war, as was the reversal of the Versailles Treaty for Germany between the two World Wars.

In a second category lie the run-of-the-mill goals towards which the everyday transactions which make up the great bulk of the work of all Foreign Offices are directed. These concern such matters as trade, tariffs, taxes, travel, finance, crime, culture, communications, visas, the interests of individuals and of corporations, all the manifold questions which inevitably arise between nations in close contact with one another. Such matters will be materially affected by a nation's orientation but they will not have any decisive influence in choosing it.

In a third group are contained those far-reaching hopes which are cherished by many states, but which in practice lie outside the capacity of nearly all. Such aims as the spreading of an ideology or religion, making the world safe for democracy, changing attitudes towards the Third World, the establishment of general free trade, world disarmament or arms control are only likely to be advanced by the greatest powers. Lesser nations may ardently desire such goals and work hard towards their achievement. Their efforts in these fields are, however, unlikely to have any decisive effect and therefore ought not to have any massive influence on their foreign policies.

When a nation has decided on the goals it can reasonably hope to achieve, those in the first or essential category will be the deciding factor in choosing an orientation.

In a changing world a country must continually review, and be prepared to revise, the aims and objectives which form the core of its foreign policy. Changes in aims may be dictated by circumstances in the international environment, by the behaviour of other states or by developments within the state itself. Goals may have to be changed or abandoned because they are no longer useful or because they are no longer practicable. It is as hard for a nation as it is for an individual to adapt to new, and especially to more straitened, circumstances, but it has to be done. Nothing is static in international affairs. The ebb and flow of prestige and power, of ambition and satisfaction, success and failure between nations is a continuous process, as are the combinations or separations of their groupings. The shrewdness with which the implications of change are judged and the skill with which appropriate reactions are implemented can be the most important factors in forming and executing foreign policy to the advantage of a nation and its people. The fortune, and even the survival, of nations depends on their vigilance and readiness to cope with new and unfamiliar circumstances.

The position of Britain in the world has changed in the last half-century, perhaps more rapidly and drastically than that of any other nation in history over a comparable period. In spite of her reputation for pragmatism and adaptability it is very questionable whether she has yet fully appraised the realities of her new situation.

The underlying principles of British foreign policy before the First World War were well stated by Sir Eyre Crowe, a professional diplomatist of the time. He wrote that 'the general character of England's foreign policy is determined by the immutable conditions of her geographical situation on the ocean flank of Europe as an island state with vast overseas colonies and dependencies . . .' The policy which he deduced from these 'immutable' conditions boiled down to two principles. The first was that Britain must maintain adequate sea power to defend her island, to control the ocean routes where her trade and shipping were paramount and to protect her empire dispersed in every continent and on which 'the sun never set'. This meant a lot of sea power. It meant having the greatest navy in the world. For a time, it even entailed the 'two power standard', the ability to dominate at sea an alliance of any two other naval powers in any part of the world.

The second principle was to keep a watchful eye that no nation obtained an overwhelming preponderance of power in Europe. In the shifting diplomacy of the Continent, Britain's influence and the threat of her naval power were available to be thrown into the balance against any combination of nations which seemed likely to achieve a dangerous degree of hegemony in Europe.

Two further concepts underlay Crowe's principles. These were that Europe was the unchallenged centre of the international world and that no power outside Europe was strong enough either in a naval/military or an industrial/financial sense seriously to affect the balance of power.

These 'core' values remained constant until the war of 1914, although the underlying concepts had already been eroded by the rise of Japan, the financial and industrial strength of the United States and the power and ambition of Germany.

When that war ended, the alliance that emerged was very different from that which had entered it. Defeated and revolutionary Russia had defected. The United States, her strength unimpaired by the struggle, dominated the scene. President Wilson, who had kept his country out of the war for so long, was in a position to dictate the shape of the peace.

The pattern which he imposed, but which the United States failed to ratify or join, was that of collective security based on the Covenant of the League of Nations. This set up a new international organisation within which some forty-four nations bound themselves forever to settle their differences peacably through discussion and agreement. Before this time such organisations had been proposed by academics, discussed by theorists and prayed for by saints, but here was one actually in being, signed by representatives of the greatest powers, those who would actually have to operate it. If it could be made to work, it was clear that this Covenant would revolutionise International Relations. The old patterns of power would wither away and peace would be maintained by discussion and reason. A recalcitrant nation would be corrected, thwarted, even punished, by the overwhelming power of the whole membership, collectively applied. Peaceful means would be used at first, but ultimately force could be met by force.

Without the blessing and leadership of the United States there was never much hope of success. Britain, with only half-hearted support from France, had neither the resources nor the resolution to do what was required, and the great ideal – for it was a great ideal – of collective security, based on moral principles, died an ignominious death. Britain and France went to war with Nazi Germany in 1939 because of their undertakings to Poland and their fear of Hitler, not because of the Covenant of the League of Nations.

The United Nations has proclaimed in its Charter of June 1945 ideals, instruments and methods not very different from those which were contained in the Covenant of the defunct and discredited League of Nations. After the defeat of Germany and Japan, however, it very soon became clear that the two greatest powers were not going to base their foreign policies on the Charter. They did not even make the kind of attempts that Britain and France had sporadically made in the League. Any hope that the United States and the Soviet Union would make the United Nations an effective authority soon died.

This means that the foreign policies of nations have again become matters of diplomacy, conference negotiation, treaty, alignment, orientation and power politics. As a practical policy no nation is able to shelter behind the benign generalities of the United Nations Charter. A country may voice, and even feel, the most sincere attachment to those principles, but it cannot base its actions on the assumption that other members will observe them in letter and spirit. The League of Nations was destroyed because the dominant power of the time disdained it. The United Nations is relatively impotent because the two strongest powers have fallen into seemingly permanent hostility.

For no nation have the conditions of international life after the Second World War been more baffling than for Britain.

When the change in relations between the super-powers became an inescapable and irreversible fact in 1948, Britain could still sustain a claim to equality of status with her much richer, much stronger American ally. Western Europe was militarily helpless and politically feeble. France was being drained of her reviving strength by colonial complications, Germany was still demilitarised by order of her conquerors. Italy, Belgium and the Netherlands had their own internal problems. Britain was still the predominant local power in spite of her growing industrial weaknesses. With Soviet communism a fully credible force commanding wide support in France and Italy, British backing for America was important and even vital to transatlantic plans for the revival of Western Europe.

When Stalin flouted his erstwhile allies by gobbling up the countries liberated by the Red Army without so much as a vestige of consultation, it seemed that Russia might have both the capacity and the appetite to make a further advance into the central body of Europe. The menace from the East may have been exaggerated at the time, but there was every reason for Western statesmen to take a cautious view. The Britain of 1948 had an unmistakable contribution to make to the American task of reviving the shattered nations of Western Europe.

Since then Britain's position in the world has declined very greatly. Her industrial production and technology have fallen behind those of West Germany, Japan and France and are almost insignificant beside the giant economies of the United States and Russia. After some centuries of 'great' and even 'greatest' power status, the scale of the post-war world has relegated Britain to an altogether lesser role.

The decline of Britain's international role, however, has not led to a rethinking of her place in the world, of the basic aims of her foreign policy nor of the orientation from which those aims can best be pursued. In the third of a century which has passed since NATO was formed, all has been done in the British tradition of pragmatism and empiricism. Problems have been dealt with as they arose and as best seemed immediately practicable within established limits. Little regard has been paid to any long-term planning of realistic policies consciously directed to the best interests of her citizens.

Post-war governments in London have too long clung to the old aura of greatness and tried to fish in the same kind of intercontinental ponds as did Salisbury and Palmerston, Edward Grey and Austen Chamberlain. This has, however unwittingly, fostered the illusion that nothing has changed.

As her credibility as a major power has declined, however, Britain has in practice been forced to nestle ever more closely under the American wing, although any hopes that the 'special relationship' could or would give any significant share in the super-power debate have proved totally illusory.

The facts are that Britain is no longer a world power, and her industrial, technological and military potential are no longer of the first rank. Sir Eyre Crowe's 'immutable facts' have vanished for ever and the time is overdue for the reappraisal of foreign policy.

The choice of an orientation on which policy should be based is largely a matter of balancing the risks inherent in each course of action against the protection which that course can bring with it. This entails analysis of the threats and dangers to Britain from which she is being protected by her policy of alliance. With this have to be considered estimates of the additional risks accepted in the alliance, and the degree of protection which is obtained.

Since the major threats in question are assumed to stem from the Soviet Union, the first step is to examine the USSR, its Empire and its behaviour as a super-power. Perceptions in this field are crucial to rational thought about the foreign policy of the United Kingdom and to this subject the next chapter is devoted.

2. The Super-powers: (1) The Soviet Union

The Union of Soviet Socialist Republics shares the centre of the world's stage with the United States of America. There are no great affairs in which Russia is not involved, no pie in which she does not have a finger.

To refer to the giant Soviet state as Russia is something of a misnomer, since ethnic Russians only constitute about half of its population and occupy less than half of its land area. When referring to the Soviet Union as a super-power, it is well to remember that, like Sparta among the Greek city-states, she is a super-power only in the military sense, making up in discipline and armaments what is lacking in cultural, industrial, agricultural and financial strengths.

The division between Russia and the rest of Europe stems, at least in part, from the schism between the Eastern and Western branches of the Christian church in the eleventh and twelfth centuries. Because of the separation, amounting to actual hostility, between Eastern and Western Christians, Russia was not exposed to the same formative and civilising influences as were the countries of West Europe. Russian culture was virtually untouched by the Renaissance and her religion was unaffected by the Reformation. She knew little of the rise of science in the seventeenth century or of the rationalising and modernising effects of the Enlightenment in the eighteenth. Even in the nineteenth century her Tsars managed effectively to hold back the currents of liberal and revolutionary thought which flowed strongly over the rest of Europe.

Distrust of foreigners, an obsession with secrecy and the repression of free opinion and communication are the Russian characteristics of which the rest of the world is most conscious. These are deeply ingrained traits which, like the huge Russian bureaucracy, have been inherited from the past but have not changed with the regime.

The Bolsheviks and their successors have always presented themselves as having overthrown an archaic and inefficient tyranny, but the last years of Tsarism were marked by some halting steps towards modernisation of industry, wider education, some social progress and even a glimmering of representative government and contacts with the outside world. The rift between Russia and the West, which was then being very slowly and cautiously bridged, has been widened and deepened since the Revolution by the suspicions and prejudices of Russian leaders, mirrored by the dislike in the West of the communist system.

More than sixty years have elapsed since that revolution, so there has been time enough to isolate a body of historical fact about Soviet actions and behaviour in foreign affairs. No magical insight is needed to formulate some kind of pattern out of the tale of actual happenings which is available for anyone to see and study. The main and inescapable conclusion is that, whether the record is considered as admirable or odious or somewhere in between, Soviet foreign policy has been remarkably consistent in its basic aims over the period. This consistency has, if anything, been intensified with the tendency of Soviet leadership to widen its base into more nearly a cabinet or committee system after the intensely personal dictatorships of Stalin and Kruschev.

The broad range of Soviet goals in foreign policy may with some confidence be identified as follows:

(1) The safety and security of the Soviet Empire

(2) The maintenance of communist regimes subservient to Russia in certain borderlands deemed vital for strategic reasons

(3) The protection of the communist regime from outside influence

(4) The maintenance of the status of super-power, in world-wide equality with the United States

(5) The avoidance of nuclear war

(6) The determination to ensure that any possible war can be decisively won, and that if it comes it will not be fought on Soviet soil

(7) The maintenance of supplies of food, raw materials and energy to the Soviet Empire

(8) The attempt to undermine and destroy democratic and capitalist regimes and substitute communist control under Russian influence or authority.

The methods which have been used by the greatest powers to prosecute their foreign policy aims have changed little in historical times and, allowing for technical developments, the way the Soviets behave now is not particularly new. What they have introduced into international life is a degree of cynicism and disregard of previously accepted standards which the traditionally minded not unnaturally find disconcerting. The essence of Soviet methods used would, however, be recognisable in any period of history and can be summarised under the following headings:

(1) The acquisition of client or satellite states in strategic positions

(2) Political and diplomatic pressures and activities

(3) The maintenance of a deterrent force equal to its greatest rival

(4) The massive build-up of every kind of armed force able to operate as far afield as possible

(5) The widespread dissemination of propaganda

(6) Subversion in vulnerable countries, sometimes combined with, or followed by, clandestine or surrogate military operations

(7) The manipulation of trade and finance

(8) The supply of armaments, sometimes on very generous terms

(9) War

All nations have national security in the forefront of their foreign-policy aims. The first seven of the Soviet goals enumerated on page 11 are 'core' aims, regarded as both vital and permanent since they are directly related to the security of the homeland. Changes in Soviet leadership or attitudes are unlikely to affect the determination of the Kremlin to pursue these core aims by any, and if necessary by all, of the methods listed.

The relentless determination and thoroughness with which the USSR pursues the aims numbered (2), (3), (4) and (6) above is often taken by non-Soviets as proof of tyranny and incipient aggression rather than as part of a congenitally excessive requirement for security. It is alarm at the methods which the Soviets use to sustain their aims rather than analysis of the aims themselves which raises so much fear and suspicion among other powers.

On the sensitive border with Western Europe, for example, the Soviets are covered by a ring of subservient states whose armed forces, trained and equipped by Russia, protect their dominant leader in the Warsaw Pact. The huge Russian forces in the area are trained and equipped to fight West of the Iron Curtain. Such 'security' is not unnaturally viewed with suspicion by those closest to it.

The maintenance of client states, nominally independent but militarily integrated with, and politically controlled by, a ruling empire, is not uncommon in history. No one should be particularly surprised, although they need not approve, that the security and fidelity to the Soviet system of these Eastern European states of precarious stability is regarded as a 'core' aim of Soviet foreign policy. The importance which the Soviets attach to the preservation of this position can hardly be over-emphasised, and the interventions in Hungary in 1956 and in Czechoslovakia in 1968 have effectively told the world that the policy is not negotiable.

The phenomenal build-up of military strength by the Soviet Union over the last thirty years is also a foreign-policy method very uncomfortable for the rest of the world. With a far smaller Gross National Product than the United States, Russia is now the equal or superior of her rival in almost every one of the vast range of sophisticated weapons of war and deterrence. Even more significant is the belief increasingly held that American superiority in equality of equipment and in the skill, training and ability of personnel has been eroded, if not ended.

This huge effort, while denying the Soviet people much in material benefits, casts a long shadow over the non-communist world. In particular, the spectacular growth in Russian sea power and long-range intervention capacity causes grave disquiet, based on the suspicion that a great land power does not acquire these particular potentials unless it has aggressive intentions.

There is, however, another side to this coin in the element of fear and suspicion endemic in the Russian, as well as in the communist, make-up. The Soviet Empire, not altogether without reason, sees itself as isolated and ringed about with enemies. Russia may be the author of her own encirclement, but encircled she is. With such a long string of military disasters adorning her past, a tendency to over-insurance is understandable. The memories of 1812, 1854, 1914, 1918 and 1942, all years when Russia was invaded from the West, die hard.

Even the great strength of the Russian Navy, with its immense force of submarines, does not look quite so unreasonable when you consider that to operate in all the seas which wash her shores Russia needs four distinct fleets. The bases of these fleets, in the Arctic, the Baltic, the Black Sea and the Pacific, are tremendous sailing distances apart and their practical ability to reinforce one another is extremely doubtful. In addition, all their exits to the oceans are relatively narrow and uncomfortably vulnerable.

The Soviet build-up, furthermore, like the American, has been influenced and swollen by a military-industrial lobby which is as potent in Russia as elsewhere, uttering dire warnings of enemy strength and nurturing fears of lethal 'breakthroughs' in technology and weaponry.

Of the other goals on the Soviet list, that of the spreading of the ideology of communism, and with it Russian influence and power, comes into the third of the categories set out in Chapter I. It is one of those wide-ranging aims which only the greatest powers can cherish with effect.

This aim, which is to change the social organisation within which the world lives, is an awesome task. However, the determinist frame within which Marx himself saw the victory of communism, and which has been accepted by Lenin and his successors in Russia, allows complete flexibility in strategy. If an end result is really inevitable, you don't have to hurry.

No Soviet leader has given any indication that the universal dissemination of communism has been erased from the list of foreign-policy objectives but, without a timescale, the urgency is naturally less than that always applied to the 'core' aims. Nevertheless, the ambition to convert an increasingly reluctant world to communism cannot be pursued by sitting on your hands and it is in furtherance of this objective that an aggressive factor often enters Russian policies and activities.

All the foreign policy 'methods' listed on page 12 above can be classed as aggressive when they are part of a campaign to impose the will and ideology of one state upon another. Operations in support of communist imperialism are continuous and few weeks pass without an indication of some Soviet move of one of these sorts, a new subversion exercise, the support of a guerilla movement or terrorist faction or an arms deal aimed at spreading influence and implanting military 'advisers'. It is in these ways that the main thrust of Soviet attempts to win the world has developed and, from all indications, will continue to develop. In spite of this emphasis, however, the first question always asked in examinations of Soviet aggression is about the use of open warfare, how it has been used in the past and how it is likely to be used in the future.

Objective examination of the record shows that the Soviets have been extremely cautious and sparing in the open use of force. Like other advanced countries, they accept the doctrine of Clausewitz that war is 'the pursuit of policy by other means' and that the risks attendant upon war are only justified when all other means to the end in view have been exhausted. Certain considerations are common to the instances when armed force has been openly used by the Soviets. These are practical, not moral, because communist morality takes the view that the end justifies the means. The overriding factors in the Soviet view of war may be listed as follows:

(1) There must be a clear, strictly limited objective of urgent and outstanding importance to the USSR

(2) The objective is not attainable by 'peaceful' methods

(3) A rapid victory is probable

(4) There must be some legalistic justification for the action

(5) The scene of action must preclude major anti-Soviet support from outside

(6) The 'war' must be unlikely to escalate

(7) The territory attacked must be likely to submit to Soviet control, entailing a substantial native communist party capable of providing a puppet administration

Virtually all these factors have been present in all essays of force initiated by the Soviets since the Revolution, although some exception must be made for the Finnish War of 1939. In that case the origins of the attack were strictly military, to obtain the use of territory for strategic purposes in the event of a German attack. No attempt was made to impose communism on Finland after the hard-won victory.

What is quite clear is that Soviet attitudes to war are not haphazard, and the rational deduction can be made that Russia will in the future only be likely to initiate wars on the principles she has used in the past. The increasing tendency to caution in the new-style Soviet leadership supports such a view.

It is fair to ask why, if this analysis is anywhere near right, it is necessary for the Russians to maintain such huge military forces. Why must they have the greatest navy in the world when they are not primarily a maritime power? Why must they match or exceed American strategic missiles warhead for warhead, launcher for launcher, megaton for megaton? Why the newly acquired capacity for long-range intervention? What is the point of all this hardware if it isn't for use? And what can it be used for except for aggression and expansion?

The answers to these questions lie partly in what was said earlier in this chapter, but also relevant are the difficulties and disadvantages under which the USSR now labours. To the outside world these are partially obscured by the screen of military strength, but they are not decreasing with the years and call for an increasing share of the attention of Soviet leaders. It is partly the failures of the Soviet system which have led to concentration on the success stories of space exploration and the armed forces.

The enormous edifice of the USSR is supported by four main pillars. These are, the Ideology on which all faith was originally based, the Economy which was expected to outstrip the world, the Empire which would bring added resources, security and trade, and Soviet military strength underpinning all.

In the first three of these spheres the last ten years have seen great changes, presenting new, and often ominous problems for the Soviet leadership.

The communist *Ideology*, foundation of the whole enterprise, has become distinctly shop-soiled. It no longer has the simple and obvious attraction which was once its great virtue. Experiment and practical trial have not proved it the infallible remedy for human ills that it seemed when Marx and Engels concocted the theory in the British Museum Library.

The passionate slogans about workers having nothing to lose but their chains, and that public ownership of the means of production, distribution and exchange is the elixir for freedom and prosperity, have lost their magic. The free world may not have coined phrases or framed panaceas any more effective, but the practice of communism has been stained and flawed by too many failures for the creed to retain the power it once had over the mass of intellectuals, idealists, trade unionists and students as well as over many ordinary people.

There is widespread disillusion in the USSR and outside with the tyrannical and militaristic face of communism. The cynicism, dishonesty and nepotism of the privileged class of Russian nationality, their place-seeking and open flaunting of advantage over fellow citizens, have undermined belief in the infallibility of the system. Even among the highest, the flame which inspired Lenin and his immediate followers has burnt low.

Decay in the ideology is not going to bring any immediate or violent reaction in Russia, but there is already an attitude of indifference and cynicism to the exhortations and promises of government which bodes ill for the future.

The failures in the Soviet Union's giant *Economy* have complemented and fed the decline in its ideology. The hopes of the original Bolsheviks that socialist planning would bring such phenomenal economic progress that the world would follow Russia into revolution soon evaporated. Five Year Plans enforced minimum consumption in the hope that capital expansion would in time bring the consumer paradise. Great efforts in propaganda, promises and police ensured control in the first, difficult phases, but the rabbit didn't emerge from the hat.

Basic to the economic structure was, and is, the collectivisation of agriculture. This was to increase food production by modernisation and mechanisation and thereby release labour for bigger and better industrial output. That didn't happen either. The murderous dispersal of the Kulaks, the peasants who formed the backbone of the countryside, is not forgotten nor forgiven. The record of the collective farms remains abysmal. Agriculture is inefficient, lethargic and corrupt. The shortfall in essential foodstuffs has to be made up by large imports of grain, often from the USA.

Total industrial production has, of course, increased, but so much is drawn into military, quasi-military and prestige projects that there has been, by Western standards, little progress in individual consumption. Any radical change of policy is unlikely because of the political necessity of retaining central control of the entire state machine.

Industrial and agricultural failure have had a striking effect on at least one output, that of propaganda. The old promises of the economic paradise have gradually faded, to be replaced by the vision of Imperial Russia, the world's leading military power, outshining the United States and spreading its influence and control to the four corners of the earth. Whether this will remain a satisfactory goal for the individual Soviet citizen and make up for the perennial shortages of goods is a matter of some doubt. This probably applies most of all to the ethnically non-Russian majority who participate little in what fruits there are of Empire.

By definition, an empire is a collection of territories inhabited by several different nationalities but controlled by a single dominant national group. The Russian *Empire*, which lies both inside and outside the boundaries of the USSR, presents many problems for its rulers. It comprises a motley array of peoples and cultures, since outside the directly ruled territory of the USSR there are various tiers of empire subject to differing degrees of Russian control, interference and influence. Countries closely involved with the Soviets range from the heavily monitored satellites in Eastern Europe, through nations such as Cuba, Ethiopia and Vietnam which are subject to varying and disputed degrees of control, to more recent and as yet unconsolidated advances in Nicaragua, Chad, Namibia and elsewhere. Some of these territories provide Russia with bases, facilities or other support in exchange for technical, military or economic assistance. Others are so far liabilities, but all need a watchful eye and at least some expenditure of resources by Moscow.

The non-Russian peoples within the USSR are more numerous than the ethnic Russians who occupy the bulk of the well-paid posts of power. The subject peoples include

Georgians, Estonians, Latvians, Lithuanians, Turkmen, Ukrainians, Poles, Ruthenians, Armenians, Uzbeks and others. Most are quite distinct in language, customs, religion, descent and appearance from the Russians. They have varying degrees of loyalty to, and often dislike of, the central Soviet state and its rulers. The minorities have an appreciably higher rate of population growth than their Russian masters. Many were quite willing to join the Germans in the invasion of 1941 and some volunteered to fight with the Waffen SS. The Russian pretence that the 'union' consists of free and equal republics with the right to secede is very thin.

This empire is an immense burden on the Soviet state. Probably no one outside the Kremlin has a real picture of the total machine of oppression needed to sustain Russian control over the subject and subservient peoples, and Communist Party control over the whole enormous empire. The armed forces absorb at least one-seventh of the Gross National Product, and to this must be added great gangs of communist party officials, KGB men, uniformed and secret police, frontier guards, supervisors, spies, agents and informers at every level at home and abroad. The true cost of the whole apparatus of state tyranny has been estimated to absorb up to one-half of the resources of the USSR. Whether this figure is accurate or not, the inefficiency and waste entailed is on a scale unimaginable to us, far higher than the drain of unemployment of which we so rightly complain.

A great part of the territory of the USSR and much of its future development capacity lie in Asia, and over Asia broods the giant shadow of China – communist yes, but immensely different from the Russian pattern.

China is still relatively backward in industrial capacity and modern technology, but she has enormous manpower and already enough missiles and nuclear weapons to alarm her neighbour. The long, desolate area (it is hardly a frontier) between Russia and China is not well demarcated and brims with actual or potential border disputes which have more than once boiled over into something very near war. The Russians find it desirable to guard, or threaten, their Southerly and Eastern flank with up to half the strength they deploy in Europe, to face the much more sophisticated forces of NATO.

After the first honeymoon when Mao Tse Tung achieved power, and in spite of periodical attempts to improve relations, there is no natural affinity and much potential cause for dispute between the two great communist powers. The independent and powerful force which China may become is something of a nightmare to the Kremlin. The obsessional fear of war on two fronts, common to central powers throughout history, now dominates Russian strategic thought.

If you add together the decline in communist ideology, the continued failure of the Soviet economy, the burden of empire and the emergence of China, the view from the Kremlin towards the promised land of communist triumph is obscured by enough problems to discourage its masters from actions likely to present them with new ones.

The performance of a great power in the past, especially in a period of rapid growth, is not a certain guide to what it will do or try to do in the future. In particular the transition from being a revisionist power to a *status quo* one is hard to chart, although it is virtually sure to occur. The study of known Soviet characteristics, aims and methods will give important and reliable probabilities, if not certainties, about the pattern of future Soviet behaviour.

It is true that in using this method, qualities of restraint and rationality are ascribed to Soviet leaders which are denied to them by the more excitable of politicians and publicists in the West. The record shows, however, that their tactics have not normally been without reason and caution.

We can expect, therefore, that the Soviets will continue to pursue the aims and use the methods we have examined. Expansion will remain part of the policy, but the retention of the gains already made will be even more important. Open warfare will only be used in circumstances either of acute danger to one of the 'core' security aims, or of the possibility of quickly, easily and safely acquiring control of an area of great strategic or economic importance to the Empire.

Propaganda, manipulation of trade, especially in oil, and the supply of arms will be used to sway or control the policies of friendly governments. Subversion, clandestine incitement to revolution and attempts to stir up and support guerilla war and terrorism will be the preferred methods where governments are hostile. The most vulnerable countries will be the poorest, the least well-governed and the most corrupt, where communist ideology can still be presented as offering something preferable to existing misery.

The disadvantages of adding to the Empire territory which is not viable economically, or which may not be trustworthy enough to contribute to defence and remain loyal to Russia, now exceed the prestige advantages. New conquests can represent a diminution rather than an increase in power which, in spite of the imposing facade, the Soviets can ill afford.

This estimate of the Soviet super-power has been made at some length because British foreign policy is currently based on a perception of Russia which regards her as a direct enemy or threat to Britain in the military sense, and which relegates to second place the more subtle and diffuse policies which the Soviets actually use to achieve their aims.

It also forgets that for Russia the centre of the world is no longer in Europe, where we in Britain are inclined from long habit to think it is. In Europe the USSR can be content with a position in which she is reasonably safe from direct attack. She can hope, and try to ensure, that her *cordon sanitaire* of satellite states will remain safely in her grip politically and militarily, sealed off from outside interference. She can conduct her propaganda, subversion and espionage operations as usual, but even while doing so the Kremlin must be conscious that the long-standing commitment to improve living standards, particularly in the Eastern European satellites, depends largely upon trade with the more advanced and prosperous countries to the West. If Russia ever succeeded, as she sometimes appears to hope, in undermining the capitalist world economy, the effect on the already precarious conditions in the Empire would be disastrous. The Eastern bloc would have to resign itself to the slow and drab task of pulling itself up by its own bootstraps.

Russian and communist expansionist hopes are now concentrated outside Europe, which no longer offers easy or even promising targets. Progress will continue to be sought elsewhere, but by tactics tempered with caution. In an empire controlling and oppressing peoples of so many different races, cultures, languages and religions, each disaffected minority is a crack, however small, in the imperial edifice. It is very unlikely that Soviet policy will set out deliberately to add to the Empire more disaffected minorities than it already has.

Gibbon wrote of the Roman Empire that finally 'the stupendous fabric yielded to the pressure of its own weight'. No one can be sure that some such process is in store for the Soviet Union, but history shows that all its predecessors of comparable size have met a similar fate.

British policy *vis-à-vis* Russia sets much store on opposition to Soviet expansionism and communist tyranny. This opposition is now expressed by military membership of the Atlantic Alliance, mainly in continental Europe. The next chapter will therefore be devoted to the leading nation of that alliance and the policies it pursues.

3. *The Super-powers: (2) The United States*

British involvement with the other super-power is much closer and our perception is not troubled by either the secrecy and duplicity which obscure Soviet activities, or by differences in culture and language. The United States operates probably the most 'open' of all known governments, yet the direction of its policy is not always easy to gauge, partly for that very reason. There can be quite violent shifts after presidential and congressional elections and there is always a baffling hiatus towards the end of a presidential term. Government is prone to influence by many well-organised and powerful pressure groups. The ear of an American President has to be open to many voices, some of which he cannot ignore. All this can make American pursuit of her objectives seem erratic and baffling to her friends and allies as well as to her opponents.

The role which the United States assumed in world affairs at the end of the Second Word War was very different from that which Britain had vacated. The task which had faced Britain at the League of Nations was to try to lead the member states to a peaceful Utopia through general co-operation. Although the enthusiasm of both the leading and the rank-and-file nations left a good deal to be desired, there was, at first at least, no active opposition to the concept of working together.

After the Second World War, however, genuine co-operation between the victors was never on offer. The temporary euphoria of friendly relations between America and the Soviet Union abruptly disappeared with President Roosevelt's death. The United States was confronted with the realisation that Stalin, who had been hailed as a brave ally against Hitler, was at best an unreliable and treacherous opportunist and at worst an implacable opponent.

It became apparent that Russian devotion to doctrinaire communism, which had been pushed into the background in war, was real in peace. This doctrine was utterly repugnant to almost all American opinion. Russian treachery in Poland and her cynical refusal to relinquish her hold on Eastern Europe were a warning in American eyes that the next step might be a dash to establish total control of the European continent. When the Marshall Plan for the revival of all Europe was coldly rejected by the Soviets and their Empire, the United States not unnaturally concluded that its task as the world's leading power could not be to promote universal and peaceful co-operation between the nations. It was to establish and maintain a power bloc strong enough to contain communist and Russian expansionism.

Britain is still a member of the Alliance which she helped the United States to construct in order to assist in the containment of Russia. Britain's foreign policy and her place in the world are now affected more by American decisions and attitudes than by what is thought in London. What, then, are those attitudes? What are the 'core' aims of American foreign policy to which Britain is inevitably harnessed by her undertakings to the Atlantic Alliance?

American interests around the world are so immense and her power, capability and wealth are so great that her influence penetrates into every corner of the globe. She has thereby acquired objectives on many subjects and in many locations. Like Russia, she is great enough to be able to pursue every category of aim with at least some hope of success. The general thrust of her policies can be summarised under half a dozen headings. These are:

(1) To maintain the security of the United States and avoid nuclear war

(2) To ensure the availability of the materials and energy needed to sustain her huge economy and her high standard of living

(3) To ensure the availability of markets for US goods and opportunities for US capital

(4) To maintain the 'Monroe Doctrine' preventing interference in the American continent by outside powers, reinforced by the 1904 amendment by Congress which claimed 'policing powers' throughout the American continent

(5) To foster the spread of American-type democracy and capitalism, in the belief that this is the best road to order, freedom and the observance of human rights

(6) To contain communism within its present limits and when and where possible, to sap and reduce its power.

These aims, like those of the other super-power, are pursued with great force and energy and with methods which may be grouped under headings not dissimilar to those used for Russia in the last chapter:

(1) Alliance with, and defence of, countries feeling the same threat from communist Russia as does the United States

(2) Financial, political, diplomatic and military support of friendly non-communist countries

(3) Maintenance of a huge strategic deterrent nuclear force

(4) War-fighting military strength, including tactical and intermediate nuclear weapons on a scale to deter attack; also maintenance of the ability to project adequate force wherever it might be needed

(5) Propaganda and subversion within the communist bloc and its supporters

(6) The supply of arms and assistance to factions and forces friendly to the US, especially in countries deemed to be at risk

(7) Official negotiation with the Soviet Union.

There is, of course, a vast difference between the ways in which these various methods are used by the responsible democracy in Washington and by the totalitarian rulers behind the closed doors of the Kremlin.

Thirty-five years ago, at the formation of NATO, American 'core' foreign-policy aims were much the same as they are today. American methods of achieving those aims have also remained the same overall but have been affected by quite radical changes to accommodate the phenomenal growth of Russian military strength and the totally different quality of the projection of Russian power.

When NATO was formed, the Soviet Union was not a world power and was not seen to be aspiring to the status of equality with the United States in that role. The perceived Russian threat in 1948 was the extension Westwards of the 'Iron Curtain' which already confined Eastern Europe under Soviet control. American containment of Russia was almost entirely achieved in the support of friendly nations and the deployment and build-up of military strength in Western Europe in aid of nations who also perceived the threat.

Thirty-five years on, American rivalry with the Soviets and the opposition of the two ideologies is on a world scale and is being pursued on the world stage. This is not to say that Europe is not still on the list of vital interests for which the United States would, in the last resort, fight. It is to say that Europe is no longer the only, or even the paramount, such interest. Even more importantly, it is no longer the interest which is seen as the most threatened. The Soviet Union is now perceived as having deliberately built up her military potential to support the projection of power over a wide range of targets far outside Europe, and this perception continues to have a radical effect on American foreign-policy thinking.

These alterations in the scene cannot fail to have a profound effect on the British situation. No free country is in such a thrall to another, more powerful, nation that it must follow blindly all changes of course made by the leader of the alliance to which it belongs. Such changes may be inevitable and necessary for the leader, but it does not follow that they are advantageous to an individual junior member of the grouping. They need to be objectively examined and assessed with due regard to the interests of each party involved.

If we examine the aims of the United States in relation to purely British interests we discover that, as is natural and proper, the 'core' aims, numbered (1) to (4) on page 24, relate entirely to United States' concerns for the benefit of her own people. Britain would not oppose these concerns, but she has neither the capacity nor any requirement to give them material support at the expense of her own legitimate national objectives.

The remaining two goals, numbered (5) and (6) on the list, fall squarely into what were described in Chapter 1 as the far-reaching ambitions only available to the most powerful nations and therefore, most legitimately, to the United States. Britain can, does and should approve these goals, but in no sense does that mean that she has an obligation to support them in the military sense if that affects her own interests or safety.

Rabid opposition to the theory and practice of communism and the perception of a threat from Russia is endemic and sincere in the United States. But although America is genuinely convinced that it is to the advantage of the friends and allies she has gathered around her to join actively in her struggle against what she regards as evil and hostile forces, she has nevertheless invited, persuaded, bribed or pressurised most of them to join the circle for reasons of American policy, not for their blue eyes. All nations act so and, in fairness to their own people, should act so. But the rule must also apply to lesser nations when they review their policies. In according all-out support, including close military alliance, to the United States, Britain must be sure that it is in the interest of her own safety to do so.

The psychological need of the United States for allies can be directly compared with the psychological need of the Russians for over-insurance in armaments. Both stem from a sense of insecurity. America, in spite of her immense strength and resources, feels insecure because a power almost equal to her own appears to her to threaten much of the world through which she has grown great and without which she cannot grow greater and richer. The competition between the super-powers for friends and allies to help in expansion, in defence and in the containment of one another's imperialism is, and is likely to be, a continuing feature of their relationship. The call of America for more support world-wide from her Alliance is becoming ever more insistent.

The importance of the policies of the super-powers for their lesser brethren is whether, and if so how, the aims and methods of Russia and the United States blend or clash with our own aims and interests, petty as these may seem to the greatest powers.

The stance of alliance ties British policy closely to the policies of America. These are concerned with the security and well-being of America, not of Britain except as a secondary consideration. British security therefore now depends, not on any circumstances which we can control or influence, but on the precarious balance of the Soviet/America confrontation. To that subject we turn in the next chapter.

4. *The Super-powers in the World*

The activities of the two super-powers are highly significant matters for the rest of the world but it is the interaction between them which most concerns the lesser nations who constitute the large majority of mankind. We all watch the super-powers with growing anxiety, deplore their sparring and vituperations, welcome their negotiations, lament the seemingly inevitable failure of each successive round. We listen, sometimes with horror and apprehension, often with the boredom born of repetition, to the insults and epithets their statesmen and publicists hurl at each other over the ether and in the political arena. All this is based on their perceptions of one another, arrived at on either side through the twin channels of ideological and nationalistic thought.

Soviet ideology tends to see the United States as a relentless, greedy capitalist society, at once the tool and the engine of huge, faceless multi-national corporations which control and manipulate half of the world's total trade, industry and finance to the detriment of its people and for the benefit of a few cigar-smoking capitalists. Russian nationalism portrays the United States as a powerful militarist nation, unafraid of unleashing nuclear war, hell-bent on the encirclement and ultimate destruction of Russia and the elimination of communism, only kept in check by the mighty counterforce of Soviet armaments and determination to keep the peace.

It would not be true to say that the American perception of the Soviet Union is quite as blinkered and rigid since there is freedom of opinion and plenty of open and animated discussion. Nevertheless, a picture of power-hungry, dogma-mad dictatorship by a few old men in the Kremlin who pore continuously over a master-plan to achieve world domination and world communism, is widespread and accepted by large numbers of Americans. It has a hold in political circles and appears in the most respectable senior common rooms. To be 'soft on communism' is still highly suspect up and down the United States.

Paranoid and dangerous as the extremes of these perceptions may seem to outsiders, the world has to live with them. Given the basic hostility that exists between the super-powers, it is hardly reasonable for self-appointed advisers to expect either side even to appear to be lowering its guard.

Hostility between Moscow and Washington does not appear only in their ideological and political differences, and in the frenetic arms race between them which is at once a symptom and a cause. There are now a number of areas, in addition to their original meeting place in Europe, in which the interests of the super-powers overlap and sometimes conflict. The determination of the Soviet Union to join the United States on equal terms as a world power has naturally increased the number and widened the content of such potential disagreements.

Conventional maps seem to show the main territories of the two to be geographically almost as far apart as they are ideologically, but closer inspection discloses the shortest distance between their mainland territories to be about thirty-eight miles. The Bering Strait between Siberia and Alaska is quite often frozen, so it would at times be possible, if uncomfortable, to pass from one super-power to the other on foot, but this type of contact is not at present a serious factor in their relationship.

The main boundary along which the forces of America and Russia, and of their respective allies, confront one another directly is the so-called 'Iron Curtain' between Eastern and Western Europe. The military preparations of NATO and of the Warsaw Pact on their respective sides of this line are such as to indicate that statesmen and strategists on both sides anticipate that a Third World War could be fought out over the old battlefields of Europe, where both super-powers have interests which they proclaim as 'vital'.

United States technology and capital have taken over and revitalised an appreciable chunk of Western European industry and services and tied them into the American trading system. America, Europe and Japan are now Siamese triplets in the highly developed world economy, joined together by the most intimate connexions through which circulates the lifeblood of the capitalist system. To part them would bring disaster to the delicate mechanism of the whole body.

American policy is based on the thesis that the European section of the system will remain stable only so long as it remains under American influence and protection. If that becomes ineffectual, a power vacuum would be left which could, and almost certainly would, be filled by Russia. The very large Soviet forces in the West of the USSR and considerable forward units deployed with the native forces of the Warsaw Pact allies are seen by the United States as evidence of Russian potential, and even intention, to effect such a conquest if opportunity arose. This would lead to the whole continent being absorbed into the communist camp under Russian military, political and economic control, totally upsetting the balance between the super-powers and going far to destroy the American financial and commercial system.

Such a disaster can, in the American view, only be avoided by the continuance of at least the *status quo* in Europe, and preferably by the pushing back of the frontiers of communism to the borders of the USSR and away from Europe proper.

To achieve even the lesser of these objectives, constant vigilance and considerable 'forward' defence is required to deter Soviet attack. This entails the fortification of the North-South axis of Europe, command of the Mediterranean and the Western Baltic and the ability to dispute the exit from the Russian Arctic into the Atlantic Ocean. The maintenance of this cordon is clear notice that the United States will not tolerate any attempt by the Soviet Union to extend its sphere of control or influence to the West by force of arms.

In Soviet eyes these dispositions appear as part of a long-term American policy of encirclement, designed to confine and hinder the USSR in its legitimate role as a world power. More urgently they are seen as a deliberate threat to the ring of countries with communist governments subservient to Russia which, as set out in Chapter 2, it is a 'core' aim of the Soviets to sustain under their tutelage and control. The terms of the Warsaw Pact enjoin that an attack on any of these countries would be regarded and dealt with as an attack on the Soviet Union itself.

The formation of NATO, and in particular the inclusion

therein of West Germany, entails for Russia the probably permanent maintenance of forces in these countries, partly to reassure their less than popular governments, and partly to deter any possibility of interference or counter-revolutionary activity from the West. These forces are maintained in an aggressive stance, apparently ready to take the offensive against the West, but this, for the Soviets, is simply the best method of ensuring that war, if it comes, will not be fought on Soviet soil.

The defection of Yugoslavia and Albania from the Soviet camp was a grave warning of the difficulties inherent for Russia in her European imperialism. The bogeys of nationalism and independence of spirit, which were not checked in time in Yugoslavia, may not be far from the surface elsewhere and the Kremlin suspects that the Americans, with their seesaw of loans and sanctions, are always on the watch for opportunities to support any urge for freedom.

Together, these are plausible reasons why a defensive position in Eastern Europe is not enough for Russia and why a strong defensive position is essential for America. An impartial observer might say that there are some grounds for the underlying suspicions which activate both sides. Perhaps there is some undefined urge, hidden in the remote recesses of Soviet ideology, to substantiate Lenin's dream of a communist Europe. Many Americans would dearly like to revive old Western promises of freedom in Czechoslovakia and Poland. But the super-powers seem to have tacitly, if not formally, come to a stalemate over their ideological territorial ambitions in Europe and the balance between them is such that neither is likely deliberately to disturb it. A question mark that remains is the old problem of Central Europe. What of the Germans?

West and East Germany are the most efficient, reliable and prosperous of the European states on their respective sides of the Iron Curtain. Each manages, albeit with some open and some concealed dissidence, to operate, without too much friction, the political system imposed upon it after the war. Is it feasible or likely that either or both of the two Germanys would upset their respective alliances by some kind of 'dash for unification'? Or by one trying to take over the other? Both are already potent industrial and military powers; together they would be a truly formidable force. May the Russians fear a West German attempt to spread discontent in East Germany with a view to 'counter-revolutionary activity'? Could America legitimately fear that, as the 'economic miracle' fades in West Germany, a significant communist element might arise there, with intent to join their brothers across the Elbe?

Either of these scenarios is implausible for the moment. The partners of one or other or both German states would have to give their help and approval, or at least active connivance. A unified and heavily armed Germany on the capitalist side would be a nightmare for Russia and even more for the satellites who have known the Germans as conquerors. A similar Germany in the communist camp would destroy the American position in Europe at a blow. With the rest of the world distrustful of even a whisper of German reunification, neither of the super-powers would consider such a development and the Germans themselves have lost much of their interest in the concept. They are likely to wait for outside circumstances to change rather than themselves try to precipitate change. The old dream of neutral and disarmed Germany may arise again one day, but it seems remote and impracticable in the existing atmosphere.

The appearance of precarious stability which broods over the 'Iron Curtain' does not alter the acute danger which subsists when two heavily armed forces face one another at close quarters and in attitudes of undisguised hostility, as is the case in Europe.

Away from Europe the most important clash between the super-powers is in the oil-rich, unstable, turbulent, fanatical and fragmented meeting place of three continents, dubbed the 'Middle East' by the West but, in some ways, now the centre of the world. The combination of poverty and riches make it an ideal target for ideologies, and the enormous oil reserves raise the possibility that the super-powers may intensify their attempts to obtain a tighter control.

The fact that their armed forces and representatives prowl around the Red Sea, the Indian Ocean, Persian Gulf and Eastern Mediterranean, acquiring bases and facilities, selling or giving away arms, searching for friends, allies, customers and clients, gives notice to the world that the fuses in the area are live.

The collapse of Iran undermined what had once seemed a strong American position, now partly restored by the acquisition of bases, allies and facilities in Somalia, Diego Garcia, Egypt and Oman, supported by a considerable fleet in the Indian Ocean and plans for rapid reinforcement, increasing the possibility of NATO involvement.

In American eyes this build-up threatens no one, but serves to reassure friendly states. The United States believes the area to be seriously threatened by Russian aggression in Afghanistan, the Horn of Africa, in Ethiopia and the Arabian Peninsula, as well as by Soviet deployments in the Red Sea and Indian Ocean.

The Russian answer is that the American presence in the region is excessive and provocative. This view is backed by a not inconsiderable Arab faction which avers that authoritarian, non-democratic governments are eroding the Arab birthright by allowing and encouraging the high rate of oil production. This lobby says, with some force, that the proceeds cannot be profitably invested in the area, and that greedy sheikhs are lining their pockets by buying shares and property in New York, London and Paris. This section of Arab opinion, not confined to the so-called 'radical' states, believes that the United States is determined to ensure the continued flow of Arab oil and sees American forces not as protection against the Soviets but as a threat to Arab independence.

It would be foolish to rule out the possibility of a clash between the super-powers in the Middle East. Here, more than in Europe, are tangible prizes, huge reserves of cheap oil and control of an important strategic area. Here are unstable regimes and politically immature peoples, susceptible to every sort of pressure by arms, money, bribery and subversion. The potential gains are enormous and the temptation for the super-powers, however cautiously, to try to tilt the balance between them is correspondingly great. The almost total reliance of many Western economies on Arab oil is well known, and America as their pivot and military leader could not tolerate any serious interference from outside which affected the supply to her clients. Problems of foreign currency, consumer goods, and even oil would be infinitely eased for the USSR and its satellites if the Middle East were to fall into the Soviet sphere. The preoccupation of both super-powers with Middle Eastern matters is growing and will continue to do so. But Arab confidence in their new-found ability to keep predators at bay and increase their own technological, military and political independence is also cautiously rising.

Britain has still some interests and influence in the area, and no more than any other Western country would she wish to see Russia preponderant in the Middle East. But American concerns are not necessarily the same as British, and if, as is becoming increasingly clear, the Arab lands are determined that neither of the super-powers shall be their master, it is no advantage for Britain to be seen as lackey in the Gulf to the United States.

Control of the Middle East was once a primary concern of Britain, but that was when the area straddled the main lifeline of the Empire and supplied the bulk of the oil for the Royal Navy on which our power structure depended. Our interest now is in peaceful and orderly development by the indigenous powers, not in the blind support of American positions with consequent involvement in US quarrels.

Afghanistan, Angola, Cuba, Ecuador, Ethiopia, Grenada, Korea, Vietnam, El Salvador. Are the happenings which have caused so much misery in these and other places signs and portents ominous for the rest of the less developed world? Or are they casual eruptions the spread of which can be contained short of a general conflagration? All have been the scenes of Russo-American confrontations to various degrees, with the employment, financing and assistance of surrogates and local power factions. All are closely compounded with problems of corruption, tyranny, poverty and injustice which, in many cases, have been increased rather than cured by outside interference.

The Soviets, supported by local dissatisfaction and misery, have often played their cards circumspectly, but there are indications that their tactics of terrorism, underground interference, subversion and propaganda may be intensified. American governments have often seen their interest as being to maintain stability rather than to risk promoting progress, and have consequently often given substantial support to highly disreputable regimes. The problems should not be underestimated and Western European efforts to indicate or support a middle course have seldom been effective. The type of moderate, liberal opinion they would like to see prominent is not available in large quantities, nor is it particularly attractive to many Latin Americans, Africans and Moslems.

The omens are not favourable for rapprochement between the super-powers around the world. The interest of lesser nations is surely not to encourage or participate in the polarisation by which local differences and struggles are made to contribute to and exacerbate super-power hostility and therefore add to the dangers of direct conflict. Medium and smaller powers, including Britain, do best not to involve themselves in super-power conflict in distant countries, but to use their influence and the weapons of aid, trade and education to build local independence and peaceful development. Such an attitude is bound to produce strains and difficulties if maintained within an alliance with a super-power.

The final aspect of the interplay between the super-powers in peacetime is that of their public or semi-public diplomacy. Talks, conferences and negotiations between them, often delayed, postponed or interrupted, have been going on since the Cold War started. There has been little enough to show in the way of concrete results and there is not much evidence that either power regards these forums and meetings very hopefully. Negotiation is, however, rather pathetically regarded by the rest of the world as the best way to avoid the holocaust which sometimes seems in store for us all if the quarrelsome giants do not stop increasing their arsenals, and if their suspicions and brinkmanship do not subside.

It has been an argument for British membership of the Atlantic Alliance that British expertise in diplomacy could exercise some influence on super-power relations. There is not the slightest sign that this has happened at any time in the last thirty years, nor is there any real reason why it should. Great issues between the greatest powers are not settled by influence from outside.

We have not been concerned here to attempt fundamental analysis or theoretical solutions of the conflicts between the United States and the Soviet Union, but only to show how Britain stands in the areas of potential dispute. We need to know in what way these areas are vital to the Britain of our time. It seems safe to conclude that in none of the matters in the super-power confrontation has there appeared any truly vital British interest which, having regard to the much reduced scale of British participation in world affairs, is protected by virtue of British membership of the Atlantic Alliance.

If, however, the United States, West Germany or any other member of the Alliance should fall into war with a Warsaw Pact country, Britain would be involved by her Treaty obligations and her membership of NATO. This suggests that the risks of Alliance may well be greater than the potential benefits, and to assess this we have to examine as best we can what are the risks of a major outbreak of war involving the super-powers, what kind of a war that might be and how Britain is likely to be affected. To these questions we turn in the next chapter.

5. What Kind of War?

The paramount aim of each of the super-powers being to avoid war, and in particular nuclear war, why is it that dread of a breakdown between them is so prevalent?

The 'anti-war' demonstrations, pamphlets, warnings, lectures, speeches, meetings, conferences, societies and campaigns so rife in countries where such activities are possible, are proof of general anxiety. If it were not widely believed that a Third World War is possible, this agitation would not go on and this book would not be being written. To paraphrase Churchill, we may say that 'Never in the history of human conflict has so much danger been perceived by so many.' The warnings and forebodings may tend to vagueness and sensationalism, with emphasis on doom and horror and a certain lack of rational argument, but they show that a sizeable fraction of the population of many countries believe that a Third World War *can* happen and that many think it will.

Since nobody wants a war, the implication is that there is danger of a slide into active hostilities through the operation of impersonal forces which elude control by normal political and diplomatic mechanisms. Mr. A.J.P. Taylor has effectively propounded the thesis that in both great wars of this century it was the inertia of events, rather than the deliberate decisions of individuals, which led to the outbreaks.

Certainly the *occasions* of those wars, the murder of the Archduke Franz Ferdinand in 1914 and Hitler's grab of Danzig in 1939, were not the sole compelling reasons for them. Quest for the real causes is still controversial, but there is readily available a longish list of facts and circumstances which tended towards conflict in each case. All of these must bear some responsibility for the outbreaks.

On pages 38-9 there is set out a 'Table of Danger' which compares some of the facts underlying the relationships between the Great Powers in 1914 (column 1) with the

The Table of Danger

1914	1939	Present Day
1. Widespread dissatisfaction with the social, industrial and political *status quo*, contributing to general instability in the international system	As in 1914, intensified	As in 1914 and 1939, much intensified
2. Militarism and pride among ruling élites; some pacifism, particularly in intellectual circles in the democracies, perceived as leading to likely weakness under attack	As in 1914, much intensified	As in 1914 and 1939, intensified again
3. System of two main alliances confronting each other; rest of the world militarily unimportant	As in 1914	As in 1914 and 1939, but confrontation wider
4. Ideological differences between the two alliances (but with Russian autocracy as odd-man-out supporting the democracies)	Ideological differences much sharper between totalitarians and democracies	Ideological differences between capitalist democracies and communists heightened by intense competition for influence with non-aligned nations
5. Ambition of a rising nation (Germany) to expand her power and possessions at the expense of present holders	As in 1914	As in 1914 and 1939, but for 'Germany' substitute 'Soviet Russia'
6. Fear in Britain and France of German ambition	As in 1914	Fear in America and elsewhere of Soviet ambition

	1914	1939	Present Day
7.	Desire for revision of previous settlement (French loss of Alsace-Lorraine in 1871)	German determination to expunge the Versailles Treaty of 1919	Russian desire for world-wide revision; Western/Japanese desire for revision of Russian-imposed setlements after 1945
8.	British/French/German/Italian squabbles on colonial questions	Less obvious but active below the surface	Russian/American distrust of one another's 'imperialism' and/or 'neo-colonialism'
9.	One major area of political instability of importance to both alliances (the Balkans)	Instability in Spain, Eastern Europe and Alsace-Lorraine	Political instability widespread – Africa, Asia, Middle East, South and Central America, Eastern Europe
10.	International arms race; Germany, already strongest military power in Europe, challenges Britain's naval lead	Western democracies try to catch up with the Axis powers	Frantic competition world-wide to increase national armaments and sell or give to others; vast arsenals of the Super-powers
11.	Inability of the 'Old Diplomacy' to cope with modern conditions, especially the impetus of mobilisations	Inability of the 'Old Diplomacy' to understand modern dictators and cope with their methods; failure of the League of Nations to make any contribution	As in 1914 and 1939; failure of the United Nations to make any contribution; failure of modern 'Conference' or 'Summit' diplomacy effectively to solve problems
12.	Fear of encirclement (war on two fronts) in Germany and Austria	Fear of encirclement in Germany	Fear of encirclement in Russia

circumstances which obtained in related fields in 1939 (column 2). In column 3 are listed corresponding circumstances of the present day. The similarity between the lists is too striking to be comfortable.

In spite of pressures it is always possible that war may be avoided or prevented. In that sense, no war is inevitable. The circumstances set out in column 1 of the table were broadly present at the time of the Agadir crisis in 1911, but war was avoided. The conditions in column 2 already existed in 1938, when war was sidestepped by the virtual capitulation of the Munich Agreement. Each of these instances indicates, however, that unless the underlying conditions are removed, or at least radically ameliorated, as they were not after Agadir or at Munich, the avoidance of war can turn out to be merely postponement.

A Third World War between Russia and America has already been 'avoided' in at least two serious crises, but the continued existence of the circumstances shown in column 3 indicates that it has not yet been prevented. It seems that we still lack the nous and the determination to make any more serious inroads into our current 'Table of Danger' than our predecessors in 1914 and 1939 made into theirs. They, too, were warned.

There is one factor which is new to our times, radically different from anything that has gone before. This is the concept of deterrence by nuclear weapons.

It is a tenable belief that, as some say, peace has been preserved between the major powers since 1945 through the existence of the so-called 'strategic' deterrents. It may be that they have served this purpose, but the thesis cannot be proved. However, the tools of deterrence have changed so fundamentally since Hiroshima and Nagasaki that it is now widely suspected that no true theory of deterrence has survived, certainly not in the sense of specific strategies of 'If you do this, I shall do that, so you'd better not.'

What deterrence now rests on is fairly difficult to say with any confidence and there are not lacking those who say it does not rest on anything. Perhaps the best analysis is that the concept now subsists uneasily on a basis of general uncertainty as to what the other side might, just possibly, do.

In addition to deterrence, the United States and the USSR

maintain, as a tool of crisis management, an implicit dialogue in which little is said but a lot understood as to the real interests and intentions of the other side. No ally, however close, takes part in this activity, which is entirely a matter between the super-powers. It is a matter of great satisfaction that this intangible safeguard should exist, but it is not altogether easy for outsiders to believe that this fragile diplomacy is a total shield against disaster.

The belief that war is impossible in the shadow of nuclear weapons has been much weakened. Partly it has succumbed to the fear that the volume of weapons and the existence of second- and third-strike capacity on both sides makes them no longer entirely credible as deterrents of conventional or 'limited' wars. Partly it has been undermined by the increasing availability of much smaller and much more accurate nuclear weapons which military men are beginning to consider as 'usable' war-fighting weapons. Wars below the 'maximum' have crept back into credibility.

The upshot has been that the concept of deterrence as the threat of unacceptable punishment being meted out to an attacker is being replaced by a variation of the older concept of the balance of power. This has often kept the peace, but never for very long. We have to face again the credibility of some kinds of war even between the possessors of nuclear weapons.

This being so, foreign policy must estimate, even if it can be only in the most general terms, how and where a war between the super-powers might be conducted and what its effects on the United Kingdom might be.

The only certainty about war is its fundamental uncertainty. All that is attempted here in gazing into the crystal ball is to demonstrate how deeply Britain, as a NATO member, would be involved in a super-power war. We shall consider the implications for Britain in such hypothetical wars under three headings, although it is clear that such headings would not be observed and a war starting in one bracket could spill over or escalate into any or all of the others. The categories we shall use are:

(1) The 'Big Bang', i.e. direct attack by the super-powers on each other's homelands

(2) Land war in Europe, either (a) conventional or (b) nuclear

(3) War elsewhere, e.g. the Middle East, Africa, a naval war

The entry by the super-powers into a direct exchange of the vast inventories of nuclear missiles permanently aimed at their respective homelands is wildly improbable. Avoiding this is the cardinal feature of both their foreign policies. It is just possible, however, that it might come through human error, misunderstanding, madness or illness. In any of these cases the result would be the same, although it is possible that a halt would be called before the ultimate holocaust destroyed the world. Technically it would be Britain's duty, under her NATO obligations, to come to the aid of her ally and pitch in with her small 'independent' nuclear force, but since this would invite immediate and total destruction of the country by Soviet weapons it seems to be an eventuality we can ignore. We would be the only nation to be in the invidious position of being a nuclear ally, with the rest of the world concerned only in trying to survive and pick up the pieces. This scenario of the 'Big Bang' is best left to the science-fiction writers, but without forgetting that it *can* become fact and that a lesser war *could* bring it about. It is not my purpose here to join the growth industry of expounding the horrors of nuclear warfare, but the sombre realities cannot be ignored.

We turn, therefore, to the type of war which, to the super-powers, would be lesser. Although they will only fight if a 'vital' interest is at stake, in this type of war it is possible that, by tacit mutual abstention, the final step of the use of the full nuclear arsenals against their homelands will be avoided. A favourite setting for this grade of war is Europe, where large forces stand in readiness on either side.

There is a basic difference between the military thought of the two big groups which face each other with undisguised hostility across the so-called Iron Curtain. On the Western side NATO thinks in terms of preventing a communist attack from overrunning free Europe. The forces maintained are barely adequate to make any serious penetration Eastward, let alone to threaten the Russian homeland.

The Warsaw Pact forces confronting them think militarily in

terms of attack. They plan for, and are equipped and ready to carry out, a giant thrust Westward, determined that if a war is fought in Europe it will be on the territory of the West.

These facts can be accepted; but they must be considered in their proper context of military-strategic facts which should not, on any account, be automatically extended into the separate area of political thinking. NATO countries can too easily believe that, because Soviet military strategy is openly based on offensive planning, this necessarily means that Soviet political intentions are also offensive.

Soviet military planning, as seen through Western eyes, is indubitably alarming, as it is surely intended to be. If deterrence fails, Russian strategy is likely to be immediate and ferocious attack. In modern terms this means a good deal more than the type of 'blitzkrieg' attack which was so successful in the Second World War.

Theorists of war have now revived and refurbished the idea of 'strategic bombardment', which was prematurely tried by both sides in the war of 1939-45. This theory was based on the selective destruction of as much as possible of the enemy's total capacity to make war, not only military installations but factories, fuel, power, transport and communications, anything which directly serves the war effort.

Until towards the end of that war, the aircraft of the time could not find, nor could their bombs destroy, their targets, and Hitler's missiles, although ingenious, were hopelessly inaccurate. The tools were inadequate and the theory was discredited but not disproven. It is likely that, with modern weapons and guidance systems, 'strategic' destruction of warmaking targets can be effective, and this strategy is now a major factor in Russian ideas of war.

The scale of bombardment can be expected to be immense and in the first quarter of an hour of war hundreds of missiles and large numbers of manned and unmanned bombers would be launched at pre-selected targets. Nuclear installations, troop concentrations, command control and intelligence, transport, airfields, weapon stores, fuel supplies, ammunition dumps, harbours, docks, railways, roads, radio and every sort of communication facility would be under attack.

A notable feature of Russian strategic thinking is that

survival of, and recovery from, the first assault is the most
crucial factor in war winning. From this it follows that the first
assault includes concentrated attacks on the enemy rear and
reinforcement areas to hamper, and if possible entirely
prevent, his recovery. Victory is to come not, as in the past,
from a series of successes which build up increasing pressure
on the enemy until he cracks, but from the application of
maximum force at the very beginning.

There is thus every indication that, in the present
dispositions of the Western Alliance, it will be Britain even
more than Western Germany which will bear the brunt of this
maximum force. Commando type landings, or even a more
concentrated amphibious attack, might be used to increase
the chaos and disruption caused by bombs and missiles.

The above is written without taking account of the nuclear
weapons held in readiness by both America and Russia for
fighting a war in Europe. It is possible, but quite uncertain,
that some sort of self-denying ordinance against the first step
into nuclear war would hold.

The Soviets have committed themselves publicly to a policy
of 'No First Use', whereas NATO presently adopts the strategy
of 'Flexible Response', which guarantees no offensive use of
nuclear weapons but anticipates their employment if required
to check an otherwise unstoppable Russian advance.

To detail probable happenings in this field is beyond the
scope of this book but, since nuclear weapons of tactical and
intermediate range and size are present in large numbers on
both sides, it is impossible to rule out the likelihood of their
use, even in the earliest stages of a war. Either side must know
that its nuclear installations are high on the target list of the
opposition and, since the numbers are limited and the
replacement rate slow, there is a dangerous temptation to use
them while they are there.

Britain, as the possessor, manufacturer and host country of
large numbers of nuclear weapons, would be under attack on a
prodigious scale in any exchange, an attack against which little
defence would be possible and from which recovery must be
doubtful.

Soviet military thought does not draw any firm line between
the use of nuclear and conventional (or, for that matter,

chemical and biological) weapons. All are regarded as tools which can be used under the direction of the political leaders to bring about the objectives of the war.

Nuclear weapons have their particular place in that, if they are used properly, they may produce the desired result of paralysis and defeat of the enemy's forces more quickly than any other method. Their use, once decided upon, would not be limited in scale. The transition to nuclear war would thus almost certainly only intensify the effort against Britain.

In thinking about a possible war on the European mainland there is a natural tendency, because of the comparative remoteness from Britain of Russia, and even of the West/East German border, to imagine that Britain would not be in the front line. In this context it is well to repeat that the Russian strategy which has been summarised includes attacking the *total* capability of their enemies to make war. All units and installations which comprise or support NATO's war-making capacity, and which are within range of Russian missiles, are in the front line.

Britain, besides the back-up facilities for her own forces in Germany and all her reserves and naval and air bases, has on her soil anything up to 200, perhaps more, American installations and units directly concerned in NATO. These are being joined by new nuclear missile facilities. All are urgent and important targets for initial Russian attack in the event of war between the super-powers in Europe.

The above is not intended to warn that the Soviets would be sure or even likely to win a war in Europe, whether or not it 'went nuclear'. Possibly no one knows enough to be able to classify the small margins which lie between spectacular success and total failure in modern warfare. A new chip, a snap decision, a chance success or an unlucky accident could sway or decide the issue. The balance between attack and defence is still in doubt. But what is not in doubt in a European war is the scale and ferocity of destruction and casualties, which would be likely to be highest along the lines of communication on both sides, with Britain probably as bad a disaster area as anywhere on the continental mainland. If they should 'win', the Russians would be too preoccupied with the problems of colonising and rehabilitating Europe to care very much whether or not they had reduced the outlying member of

NATO to that radioactive desert which they would wish to avoid producing on the mainland.

Politico-military thought is now inclined towards the possibility of war between the super-powers erupting elsewhere than in Europe. In such a case both sides may be expected to abide by the two classic doctrines of Clausewitz, that war is the continuance of policy by other means and that the first rule of war is to define and limit the political objectives for which it is fought. Both powers will, therefore, try to use only the degree of force necessary to achieve their objectives.

In an 'outlying' war, most probably about resource usage, they will, at first anyway, try to isolate the area of hostilities. Each will make efforts to restrict the struggle to the gain of limited objectives. There can be no certainty that these efforts will succeed, but both sides will hope to avoid the ignition of a separate war in Europe or the 'ultimate' attack on one another's home territory. The difficulty of restraint when both sides have only entered the war because they saw 'vital' interests as being at stake is obvious. They will fight for 'vital' interests until one or both perceives some imminent danger to other, even more 'vital' interests. We can only guess at what rung of the ladder of escalation they will stop.

Russia will quite probably prefer, and may be able to choose, that a 'resource war' turns first to the sea. Such a war could be dispersed all about the world, with each side intent on attacking the most prominent weaknesses and most vital arteries of the opposing alliance wherever they might seem vulnerable.

A sea war between the super-powers would be the widest-ranging and most intensive naval war ever waged. The mutual inhibitions against starting a full-scale land war would increase the scale of the resources and effort devoted to the sea. The Soviet and US Navies would have first call on their countries' immense war potentials, and the allies and satellites would be expected to throw in everything they had in ships, aircraft, scientific skills and men. Many wars have been won by the exercise of sea power, but this has usually been the result of a land power not being able or resourceful enough to overcome an opponent exercising superior power and mobility by sea. Never in the chequered history of warfare have the two greatest powers in the world elected to decide their fates entirely by war at sea, but there is no reason to suppose it cannot happen. This is not to say that there would be no action by land, but that land war would be subjected to the requirements of the sea war. Land operation, as also the very vital air, electronic and space wars, would all serve the sea as the vital arm. The super-power which won the sea war would hold its opponent, and its opponent's allies, helpless. Both super-powers must be aware that this is the only way a war between them can be settled without total destruction on both sides. To question a sea decision by recourse to the strategic nuclear option would raise all the arguments against national suicide, and even in the circumstances of imminent defeat at sea, it is still little credible that anyone will order the use of weapons which can only invite his own destruction.

The strategies of the sea war would be very complex, since all arms of naval and air warfare would be used by both sides, and both sides would be concerned to attack and defend simultaneously.

The US and its allies would have the more difficult task since they would be under the necessity of keeping sea lanes open for their merchant shipping, whereas the Soviet has a much lesser requirement for overseas trade and resources, and would be operating on internal lines, albeit of immense length and doubtful efficiency. The United States would be concerned to defend whichever sea lanes she saw as essential, basically the oil routes. The only strategy would be, in the Nelsonian phrase, 'to seek out and destroy the enemy'. A very important part of this would be to try to seal, or at the least make very hazardous, the four relatively narrow exits to the oceans by which the Soviet ships and submarines must pass from their bases to the open sea. About these exits air and sea fighting would be particularly intense.

Soviet aims would be to deny the freedom of the seas to America and her allies, preventing supplies and reinforcements from reaching areas of conflict. In particular the Soviets would try to impede the passage of oil and strategic material within the American Alliance. They would essay, by worldwide action, using submarines, missiles and aircraft, to cut the sea lanes without which the Alliance could not continue the war.

The scenario is, of course, oversimplified, but in essence the aims and strategies of both sides cannot be much other than as suggested. Both would be simultaneously on the offensive and defensive, the essential contest being an enormously inflated version of the age-old concept of struggle for command of the sea. Command of the sea now includes the ability effectively to control the air in areas to which shipping must converge, freedom to operate in space for information and communication, and the ability to deny the underwater to the opposition. A great, perhaps crucial, advantage in naval warfare lies with the side which has the use of land-based aircraft within range of sea areas important to the fleets.

The full implications of this concept are complex, but one certainty is that land areas from which air cover can be provided over strategic passages will be among the earliest targets in a sea war. The range and increasing accuracy of missiles, ground-based or airborne, nuclear or conventional, have revived the theory of strategic bombing, especially with the new designs of small 'area' weapons which are expected to be lethal against such targets as airfields, docks and repair facilities. It is hard to imagine the super-powers, locked in a struggle to the death at sea, refraining indefinitely from using some of their huge and varied arsenals of weapons for attacking harbours, repair and radio facilities, airfields etc. which were endangering their operations on, above and below the surface of the oceans. Such land targets would soon be in the very forefront of the battle, and attacks on them would be determined and prolonged. This would not necessarily, or even probably, predicate escalation into full-scale land war in Europe or elsewhere, certainly not into an intercontinental missile exchange on a great scale. It does bode ill, however, for those areas of both alliances which have high strategic value in the maritime sense.

The situation of Britain, threatening from her Northern harbours the main Soviet exit to the Atlantic, the only direct Russian access to the open seas of the West, would be crucial to both sides. Control of this exit could decide the fate of a Russian/American war in which naval power was the preponderant factor, and both sides could be expected to fight for it with implacable vigour. Britain within NATO could not fail to be a primary target for the Soviet Union, whose survival might depend on access to the Atlantic from Murmansk.

It is quite probable that Russia's tactics in any war fought with a predominantly naval strategy would be to knock Britain out of the struggle at an early stage. Few North Sea oil installations would be likely to survive the first few days, nor many of the refining and storage units. The relative ease and accuracy with which such installations and, of course, harbour, transport and power operations can now be attacked by missiles would make Britain, as a member of the Western Alliance, the most profitable initial target in a naval war between America and Russia.

If the war were nuclear, and Britain used her nuclear pop-gun on a Russian city to try to deter attacks on NATO installations, the Soviets, with their immense nuclear armoury, might well consider that the British attack justified the, for them, convenient ripost of the virtual annihilation of the island. Our allies could neither save nor succour us.

There are other scenarios which would fit the possibilities in an armed conflict between the super-powers, but most of them could be expected to conform in general with the suggestions which have been set out here. For Britain it is not hard to see that the least lethal of the disasters, which is also the least likely, might be the direct battle of the giants attacking one another's homelands. If that happened, which it almost certainly won't, and if it stopped short of 'Mutual Assured Destruction' killing us all, which it probably would, Britain might just possibly escape most of the punishment she would have to endure in a 'lesser' war.

There is no conceivable 'lesser' war between the super-powers which can be visualised without Britain having to absorb a high proportion of the first shock of the Russian strategy of immediate mass attack.

This 'place of honour' which Britain occupies in an updated NATO prompts a general examination of Britain's defence arrangements within this framework, and to this we turn in the next chapter.

6. *British Defence: The Status Quo*

Britain's defence posture has changed, gradually but completely, from that of the pre-war era. Then we were a world power, responsible for the defence of overseas territories and communications as well as of our own islands. At that time, partly in the name of economy, partly in what was taken to be the pursuit of peace, the armed forces were starved of the equipment they needed and what was available was consequently deployed with little heed to any specific strategic doctrine.

Things are very different now. We spend more in absolute terms on armaments than any other major Western European country – more per head of population and more as a proportion of Gross National Product. The spending is based on a definite strategic policy repeatedly emphasised in government statements on defence.

That policy rests on the doctrine that the main security threat to Britain is the nuclear and conventional forces of the Warsaw Pact led by Soviet Russia, and that defence against that threat is best assured by the forward defence of Western Europe under American leadership. The doctrine was formulated in the late nineteen forties and has undergone no appreciable change since then. The main effort is concentrated on the defence of the Eastern frontier of the Federal Republic of Germany, where Britain is called upon for a considerable effort.

When the policy was first proposed in 1949, Britain was the strongest military and industrial power in Europe. Her forces were still occupying Germany, which was without any armed forces. Without active British involvement the defence of the West German frontier at that time would have been unthinkable, since none of the mainland countries had rebuilt its defence capability.

In spite of the decline in our industrial power and the

spectacular increase of that of all the continental countries, the task of defending them is still with us. The British defence effort, as manifested in the 1984 White Paper, is planned and formulated around the indefinite continuance of the policy.

Defence is often assessed by viewing each of the three fighting services separately, but the general picture now is probably clearer if the five main functional divisions of British defence are listed. These are:

(1) Army and Royal Air Force units in West Germany under NATO command, with lines of communication and reserves
(2) Royal Navy, mostly assigned to NATO
(3) Strategic nuclear deterrent
(4) Defence of the home base
(5) 'Residual' and miscellaneous functions

It has been the policy of successive British Governments that British security depends entirely on NATO, and the 1984 White Paper underlined this, saying that 'some 95% of our total defence budget is devoted directly or indirectly to Alliance tasks'. This staggering figure is presumably arrived at by including the home base as part of the NATO area, although there appears to be no non-British contribution to its defence.

The British Army in Germany includes no less than thirteen Headquarter Units, thirteen armoured regiments, fifteen artillery regiments, seven regiments of engineers, thirteen battalions of infantry and its own air support. The force comprises more than half the effective fighting strength of the British Army. It stands in far forward positions with little support in depth and has long lines of communication with its home base. It is separated from England by two formidable water barriers, the Rhine River and the North Sea. It contains the best of our fighting equipment, and, although some is inevitably not of the latest design and the supply of some items such as anti-tank missiles and even basic ammunition is probably below the highest modern requirement, it is generally believed that it is one of the finest fighting forces in the world. The difficult task of maintaining keenness and morale in defence of a foreign country seems to be effected with continuing success.

The total army strength in Germany is about 55,000 men and women, to which must be added the resources necessarily employed in keeping up supply and communication on the long line homewards. On mobilisation the British Army of the Rhine would be doubled in strength, a very high proportion of regular and trained reserves being earmarked for immediate reinforcement. 70% of the British Army would then be deployed for the defence of the German frontier.

The Royal Air Force has twelve squadrons in Germany together with the appropriate staff formations, air defence units, airfield defences, communications, logistic support and radar. On mobilisation these units would be reinforced from regular sources in Britain and possibly by auxiliary and reserve personnel. Virtually the whole of Strike Command located in Britain and comprising all the Royal Air Force's operational units of bombers (some nuclear), fighter bombers, interceptors, maritime and transport aircraft are available to NATO and their operational training is based on NATO.

The squadrons in Germany are equipped with the best British aircraft presently available, Phantoms, Buccaneers, Jaguars, Harriers, and increasingly with the new Tornado. Their duties are the normal ones of reconnaissance, ground attack, interception, strike attack, infantry and tank support. The new Nimrod British Early Warning (Airborne) System is to be integrated with the NATO Early Warning system as a British contribution to the total.

The rapid development of modern weaponry entails continuous re-equipment and the Royal Air Force has much new hardware in the pipeline, aircraft, missiles, radar, radio and air-to-air refuelling, practically all of which is in support of NATO. Land-based fleet defence in support of the Royal Navy and other NATO fleet units is being upgraded.

British forces in Germany are maintained in a true front-line role, ready with American and West Germans alongside them, to take the first brunt of a Warsaw Pact attack on the Federal Republic. They are situated in a foreign country where they are no longer particularly welcome. As is usual with forces serving outside their home country, they live in national enclaves, taking little part in the life of the country around them. In exchange they receive some luxuries and privileges denied them at home, but their situation is by no means totally enviable.

The lines of communication with the home base are long and expensive to maintain. The paraphernalia of home leave for all, with travelling time, the support and supply on British lines of wives and families, schools, hospitals and recreation facilities in a foreign country are a constant strain on fuel and transport facilities, personnel and money. It is almost impossible to compute the true cost to Britain of maintaining its most important front-line defence units in a constant state of readiness so far from home. In many ways it is new and uncharted country because service abroad in peacetime has previously meant either policing, occupation or showing the flag, relatively pedestrian duties which did not entail maintaining in combat trim highly sophisticated equipment and skilled personnel.

A further British commitment to the defence of mainland Europe is that of assistance to Norway in emergency, although it is very difficult to see how this could be carried out within any resources likely to be available.

No one can doubt that Britain has proved her absolute faith in NATO as her sole shield. She has assigned practically the whole of her ground and air forces to the assistance of the United States in the defence of the mainland of Europe. There is hardly a man or a bullet in the regular or trained reserves of the Army and Royal Air Force without a role in preventing that Soviet break-through into Europe which was the bogey in 1949 and is apparently still a prime expectation, judging by the continual calls for more and better of everything by the allied military planners.

This is not all. Britain still maintains a sizeable Royal Navy, the largest and best of the European powers, and virtually the whole of it is assigned to NATO. Its primary role is that of controlling and keeping clear of enemy submarines and raiders the Western Approaches and, in conjunction with American forces, the Eastern Atlantic. Only if this is achieved can the free flow of American supply, communication and reinforcement, considered essential for any campaign in Europe, be maintained.

To carry out its NATO tasks the Royal Navy has a substantial anti-submarine (ASW) warfare component, with three ASW aircraft carriers capable, as was shown in the Falklands episode, of operating far afield. There are twenty-seven attack submarines capable of ASW as well as of hunting surface ships. Twelve are nuclear-powered and capable of staying at sea, and if necessary staying submerged, for very long periods. But although great resources have been expended by the United States, Britain, other NATO countries and the Soviet Union on research into ASW, and very considerable progress has been made, there is no evidence as yet that the submarine has been mastered by the formidable efforts arrayed against it. It is ill news for surface ships that the efficiency of the convoy system, once their salvation, is widely believed to be much under suspicion.

In her surface fleet Britain maintains some dozen guided missile destroyers and a considerable fleet of general-purpose frigates, variously equipped with guns, ASW capacity, anti-aircraft and surface missiles and helicopters. About one-quarter of these, as well as ten of the diesel-powered submarines, are over-age, but are still regarded as operationally useful.

The Royal Navy can no longer play a substantial part in the protection of trade routes across the world, a task traditionally only within the capacity of the greatest powers. Nor is there apparent any great effort devoted to the defence of our coasts or inshore waters against raiders or invasion, contingencies which are not regarded as a likely menace. All reliance is based on the efficiency of deterrence and the successful land shield against attack on West Germany.

The third leg of the British defence effort, the so-called 'strategic' nuclear deterrent, consists of four 'Resolution'-type submarines, nuclear-powered and each armed with sixteen 'Polaris' nuclear missiles of considerable power and moderate accuracy. When updated with 'Chevaline' warheads they have more striking power, but are still in no sense war-fighting weapons and can only be used for threatening or destroying urban or area targets. They are to be replaced by four larger submarines, fitted with the more powerful and considerably more accurate 'Trident' missiles. These units, assigned to NATO as part of the agreed British contribution to the Alliance, are primarily for use on behalf of NATO. Some defence thinkers regard them as an insurance against any idea that the United States might not be prepared to use its own strategic deterrent on behalf of Europe. These missiles can, if so required, be used by Britain on her own behalf. This is not the place to argue the worth of the British nuclear deterrent in the context of the defence of Britain in NATO. It does not absorb a very high proportion of the British defence effort and it seems to be acceptable to NATO as part of the British contribution. This is not altogether surprising, since retribution for its use might be expected to fall entirely on Britain. The countries of Western Europe, in accepting whatever protection is afforded them by the 'British' deterrent, may hope that they are getting its deterrence without letting themselves in for a Soviet attack in return.

The nuclear deterrent force, and its renewal, were the only sections of the British defence effort left untouched by the 'Nott' review of 1981, and successive Governments have seemed convinced of its useful function within NATO.

After the 'strategic deterrent' (some would say a long way after), comes that element of the British defence structure charged with the actual defence of the island, the homes and factories, harbours and airfields, cities and fields and, of course, people.

By far the greater part of the British forces stationed in the United Kingdom are earmarked for the reinforcement or bringing up to war establishment of the contribution to NATO. After mobilisation when, hopefully, the great exodus to Germany has been safely effected, there are half a dozen infantry brigades for actual home defence. Strike Command of the Royal Air Force is responsible for the defence of British airspace as a section of the total NATO area. There is likely to be more air effort available for the essential support of the naval commitment at sea than there is for the land area of Britain.

The observer cannot fail to be forcefully impressed by the total faith of defence planners that the only conceivable peril against which Britain's defences have to guard is a replica of the happenings of the 1939-45 war. Then a formidable power from the East attacked and conquered the continent of Europe as far as its Western seaboard and then, and only then, stood ready to invade our island. The Maginot Line of the time was not competent to check the invader. Can we be sure that the update of the Maginot Line on the Eastern frontier of Germany will hold? The answer to this question seems to lie in an abstruse maze of theory about deterrence, flexible response and American intentions.

The large contingent of American forces stationed in Britain do not, contrary to some impressions, take any part in the defence of our island. They serve, support or operate with either United States forces assigned to NATO in Europe or Amerian commitments worldwide.

The British Government has lately admitted the inadequacy of our home defence and announced some steps towards strengthening it, at least in the air. Progress is not likely to be exactly precipitate.

An interesting footnote to the home-defence story is the 'private enterprise' campaign for a Local Defence Volunteer Force mounted by Admiral Lord Hill-Norton (former Chief of the Defence Staff) and some distinguished collaborators, on the grounds that the country is totally unprepared for the real possibility of direct attack.

The last of the five frames in the British defence scene is the 'residual' commitment to interests outside the United Kingdom, mostly responsibilities to those awkward relics of Empire which have not been big enough for independence or are unwilling to change their allegiance. In various ways Gibraltar, Cyprus, Hong Kong, Belize, Diego Garcia and the Falkland Islands are in this category. The last named has been a disaster area for defence planners and seems likely to remain so pending any political initiative. The scale of the others is relatively small and, difficult as political solutions may be, they are fairly unlikely to present major defence problems.

There is one, at present somewhat indeterminate, addition which should be noted. This is the contribution which has been promised to the support of the United States Long Range Rapid Deployment Force. It seems that, for reasons of manpower shortage and financial stringency, the contribution is likely to be small. Nevertheless, the deeper implications of the commitment could be wide and serious, by implying support for United States' policy anywhere in the world.

This digest of Britain's defence arrangements as dictated by the foreign policy of alliance shows, to the justified regret of many British people, that there can be virtually nothing ever likely to be available for more than a token contribution to any United Nations peacekeeping force, however worthy the cause.

It must also be added that it is already difficult, and will soon be impossible, for Britain to maintain the scale of the present effort in all of the categories listed. Neither improvement in finances nor a better industrial performance is in the least likely to enable Britain to cope with the requirements, including new and highly sophisticated equipment, which will inevitably be called for in the next few years. Unlike the Red Queen, we shall not be able to run fast enough even to stay where we are.

There is no intention here to criticise these arrangements in detail. Apart from the controversial renewal of the so-called 'strategic deterrent', which some see as immoral, expensive and unnecessary, there is little alternative to what is now done so long as defence is based on the foreign-policy orientation of alliance and the commitment to defend West Germany from attack or disturbance in the East.

There has lately been a noticeable tendency in the Commission of the EEC and in the European 'Parliament', which has little useful function at present, to moot some kind of 'European' control in defence matters. These moves are presumably intended to try to remove British defence direction and policy even further from British control and to tie Britain even more closely to the endemic instability in Eastern Europe and the support of West German and American policies there. British defence arrangements and planning are fully geared to our status as a satellite of the United States and we no longer have any real capacity to defend our island. This is despite the maintenance of 325,000 men in the armed forces, supported by 240,000 civilians and some rather shadowy reserve organisation. The Defence Budget for 1982-3 was over £14 billion and will rise to over £17 billion for 1984-5 and over £18 billion for 1985-6. These costs make up about 5.4% of total British Gross Domestic Product, compared with 4.2 per cent for France, 3.4 per cent for Germany and 2.8 per cent for Italy.

If the British stance within NATO is fraught with dangers and disadvantages apparently greater than the benefits obtained, we have to ask ourselves three basic questions about foreign policy. Is membership of the Western Alliance, under the leadership of America and in confrontation with the USSR, either the only possible or the best policy available to Britain?

Does it accord with the principle that the first requirement of foreign policy is to ensure the safety of the nation? Is there any alternative orientation available?

The only practical alternative is that of military non-alignment. This would mean standing on our own feet as a medium-sized power no longer capable nor desirous of playing a leading part on the world stage, and no longer feeling it in the interests of our people to be militarily involved in the battle of the giants.

The remainder of the book will be devoted to considering whether adoption of this policy, which would be totally without prejudice to our whole-hearted support of the United Nations Charter and of the principles of individual and national freedom, would be of advantage to Britain and the world. The stance is maintained by others of the industrially developed nations of Europe and in the next chapter we shall see how they have fared.

7. *Aspects of Neutrality*

Some nations, as I pointed out in Chapter 1, have adopted as a policy the determination not to get involved in war. The attitude is variously described as neutrality, neutralisation, neutralism or non-alignment. The different shades of meaning are not always either clear or consistent, but the essential aim is to avoid being drawn into war. The method is to keep as far away as possible from the quarrels, threats or promises of other states which may lead to war.

If Britain is to consider the adoption of a stance of military non-alignment, she will need to draw on the experience and expertise of existing neutral states in order, hopefully, to emulate their successes and avoid their failures.

Neutrality, as it was defined by the Hague Convention of 1907, only applied in time of war. A neutral nation gave no military help to either side and preserved as much impartiality as possible between the warring states. There has been a natural tendency for neutrals to sell 'contraband' and obtain high prices because of the scarcity of many goods in wartime, so neutrality, at first sight a high-minded and admirable stance, has often seemed in practice to be tainted with a degree of profiteering. Hard-pressed belligerents have regarded neutrals as grasping and greedy opportunists, oblivious of the high ideals for which the war was being fought and determined only to make a fast buck.

The concept of *'neutralisation'* is more far-reaching. A country with this status will have given formal international undertakings in peacetime to be neutral during any conflict, not to allow foreign troops or bases on its soil at any time, nor to make any warlike arrangements or preparations in collaboration with any other state. The defence forces of a neutralised country may be regulated in size or quality by the treaty which defines its neutrality. These undertakings and obligations may be underwritten, approved, and have sometimes been imposed, by other states signatory to the treaty. In exchange, the neutralised state receives guarantees that its territorial integrity and neutral rights will be respected in peace and war. Such undertakings have not always been honoured, and it is hardly necessary to say that neutralisation of a state is not often guaranteed by great powers unless they see visible advantage to themselves.

The neutralisation of Belgium, for instance, was promoted by Britain as a way to prevent control of the Low Countries passing to either France or Germany. The Soviet Union exacted the neutralisation of Austria as the price of ending the post-war occupation, and reaped the considerable benefit of dividing NATO's Northern front from its Southern.

Neutralism has a less formal status, consisting of the declaration by a country of its intention voluntarily to adopt a stance similar to neutralisation. It may be endorsed by other powers, but this, of course, is equally voluntary. The word neutralism has, unfortunately, become debased by 'hawks' in the Western Alliance, who use it in a derogatory and inaccurate sense.

Non-alignment is commonly used to describe the policy of those states which refuse to commit themselves in any military sense to either side in the seemingly permanent confrontation between the two major blocs. The stance need not extend to the diplomatic or economic fields and does not rule out a general sympathy with one side or the other, nor the lending of support on individual issues. It does imply independence of any form of standing obligation.

The most prominent states which presently maintain the stance in Europe are Switzerland, Sweden, Austria, Yugoslavia and Finland. We shall make short examinations of the circumstances and behaviour of these five, with a glance at one 'failed' neutral, Belgium.

The neutrality which *Switzerland* had practised for many years was recognised and guaranteed by the Great Powers at the Congress of Vienna. One hundred years later, in the First World War, Switzerland found herself entirely surrounded by belligerent countries, all fighting for their lives. She managed to retain her neutrality in spite of pressures on the conflicting sympathies of her French-, German- and Italian-speaking people.

This was the first major war in which the International Red Cross, based in Switzerland, commanded universal respect and appreciation. The events of 1914 undoubtedly raised the standing and prestige of Swiss neutrality in the eyes of the whole world.

Paradoxically, the Swiss who emerged from the shadow of that war with the reputation of the world's most peace-loving nation, found great difficulty in accommodating their institutional neutrality within the framework of the new peacekeeping intentions of the League of Nations.

Switzerland did join the League, but with misgivings at the idea that, as a member state, she might be required to allow the passage of troops through her territory and, in the last resort, take warlike action on behalf of the League against an aggressor.

These ideas had seemed admirable in principle when they were formulated, conjuring up a vision of the whole world being willing to oppose a proven aggressor, and, if ultimately necessary, join in a universal crusade against him.

However, the Swiss, having frontiers bordering on Germany, France, Italy and Austria, all nations at that time with no great reputation for keeping the peace, saw themselves, if the Covenant were invoked against any of their neighbours, as only too likely to lose their prized neutrality and to bear the brunt of war for no reason other than their proximity to the participants. The Swiss, on joining the League, asked for, and obtained, exemption from this responsibility.

Later Switzerland also obtained release from the obligation to participate in economic sanctions. She had been such a dilatory and unenthusiastic participator in the sanctions imposed on Italy in 1936 that this release was little more than a formality. However, since she bordered the European states then most likely to disturb the peace, Switzerland was well entitled to feel that her national security would be at risk if she were compelled to take a major part in the application of sanctions against one or other of her powerful neighbours.

By the time of the outbreak of the Second World War the League of Nations had lost all credibility and Switzerland had reverted to her normal stance of absolute neutrality. It is noteworthy that she took the precaution of mobilising her forces and manning her defences on 28 August 1939, some days before Hitler's attack on Poland and before either France or England had made any major move towards mobilisation.

After the German conquest of France in 1940, Switzerland was effectively encircled by the Axis powers. All communication with the outside world had to pass through or over Axis-controlled territory. German pressures grew stronger and internal support for the local Nazi party began to constitute a significant threat to Swiss integrity and independence. At the height of German power the Swiss government had to tread very carefully indeed to check the sort of subversive operations which the Nazis had employed so successfully in Austria, Czechoslovakia and Poland. The threat of a German-supported Nazi coup was inherent in the pressing invitations to Switzerland to join publicly in Hitler's 'New Order' in Europe.

Although she permitted her nationals to fight with the Nazis as volunteers (two-thirds of the Swiss are German-speaking), she made no other substantial concessions and Switzerland emerged from the ordeal with her neutrality image not much tarnished.

Switzerland takes an active part in international affairs and is accorded great respect for the experience and skill with which she conducts the diplomacy of neutrality. While participating vigorously in many United Nations activities, especially with the technical agencies, she stays out of the politics of struggle and confrontation but is willing to 'render services for which other states are sometimes less suitable, such as mediation, humanitarian actions . . . the extension of the scope of international arbitration, participation in the work of international organisations and control commissions etc.'[1]

Swiss neutrality is supported by the ability and determination to fight if necessary for the preservation of the national existence, using the policy known as 'dissuasion'. Such a small country cannot hope to defeat any possible attacker, but it can demonstrate that an attack would not bring rewards commensurate with the price which the defence by the whole population would exact. An attack would be met by a carefully

---

[1] Quoted from the Swiss official publication, *General Defence* (1976).

prepared defence, conducted with modern weapons and the advantage of mountainous terrain. If necessary, guerilla operations and civil non-cooperation with the invader would follow. There would be a formidable bill to be weighed against whatever advantage the attacker had hoped to gain from his aggression.

Every Swiss is legally bound to do military service and the country's defence philosophy is based on a 'militia' system which can effectively produce, quite literally, a nation in arms.

There is a small highly professional element which provides a nucleus of instructors, officers, NCO's, aircrew and General Staff. 30,000 recruits join annually for their initial training of seventeen weeks and they are then assigned to units in the 'Auszug' Corps, operational units of the 20-32 age group. These form the 'manoeuvre' mobile divisions, the anti-aircraft units and the technical arms of the Army and Air Corps. At 32, men transfer for ten years to the 'Landwehr', less mobile combat units, manning permanent defence positions. For those aged 43-50, duties are more in the nature of guard, logistic and support functions, but the men are still under arms. So for thirty years of his life every Swiss man is an active soldier. After the age of 50 he will normally transfer to the civil defence organisation which is actively operated by the civil authorities.

Switzerland reckons to be able to field a trained army of more than half a million men within forty-eight hours of alert. This is no idle boast: the mobilised units would have a high standard of training, good equipment and intimate knowledge of the duties they will undertake and of the terrain they will defend. No invader, however powerful, could expect a walkover.

Switzerland has now no obvious enemy, but retains the memory of the Nazis, who might not have been deterred by her neutrality, and of Napoleon, who was not. At the crossroads of Europe, a great power or one of the great alliances might always be tempted to use Swiss territory as a short cut, or for an outflanking movement. So, in spite of Swiss preference for the Western way of life and institutions, defence plans are without favour to any side. The army and air force are briefed to defend Swiss territory from the periphery and in depth against attack or intrusion from any quarter. For air defence there is a small permanent force, for which much of the aircrew training is done with the co-operation of the national airline, Swissair. No one would pretend that the country is, or ever could be, invulnerable from the air. The air effort, like the ground-defence effort, is directed to dissuasion, the exacting of a high price for attack.

The Swiss defence planners take the view that a direct attack by 'weapons of mass destruction', or even blackmail by threat of such attack, is unlikely and is not their greatest problem. Their preparations in this sphere, which are more advanced than in most countries, are directed towards surviving the fall-out effects which the employment of nuclear weapons outside Swiss territory might bring. Every dwelling built in Switzerland since 1971 is by law protected from nuclear hazards.

The lesson of Swiss neutrality, which has preserved itself intact since Napoleonic times and dates back much further, is two-fold. Swiss insistence has brought international recognition, respect and belief in the integrity of the concept. But it is even more important that this is backed by strength in arms and above all by strength in spirit. The saying that in war the moral is to the physical as three is to one is doubly true in the strategy of a neutral. Paradoxically, peace may prove an enemy. If rich Switzerland succumbs to the lethargy and weakening of will which has so often afflicted rich nations at peace, she will be vulnerable to the weapons of political, psychological and terrorist subversion which could be the preludes to the undermining and destruction of her neutrality. If, however, she maintains her political coherence and military resolve, that neutrality seems likely to remain her shield in an uncertain world.

Swedish neutrality is not recognised or formalised by international agreement, but is as strongly upheld by national sentiment as is that of Switzerland. It is the central factor in Swedish foreign policy and a powerful one in the internal workings of the country.

Historically Sweden has a great tradition of military valour and skill. The armies of Gustavus Adolphus, the Swedish hero-king of the seventeenth century, revolutionised warfare and saved the cause of Protestantism in Europe. At the Treaty of Westphalia, which ended the Thirty Years War, Sweden was the greatest power in North Europe and the champion of the Lutheran cause against the power of Pope and Emperor. She controlled the Baltic and much of Germany. Gustavus's successors Charles X, XI and XII were warriors all and their armies had phenomenal triumphs in Europe, notably against the Russia of Peter the Great.

Sweden, however, was a small and poor country and never had a base strong enough to sustain these extraordinary exploits. In the eighteenth century, she prudently retired to her national territory, abandoning her one-time design to keep the Baltic a Swedish lake, which had entailed controlling the South Baltic coast. As a small nation with difficult geography, bad communications and small material resources, her military achievements had been astonishing, but in the end they had brought her little except glory.

During the nineteenth century the Scandinavian lands lay outside the sphere of the shifting alliance structures of the European great powers. Sweden took no part in the race for colonial expansion and remained aloof from the uneasy relations between the main continental nations.

In 1914 Swedish sympathies lay more with Germany than with Russia, her traditional enemy, but she remained doggedly neutral through the years of war, probably more irritated by the British blockade than by the German submarine campaigns. At Versailles she became a founder member of the League of Nations. She maintained her neutral posture throughout the inter-war years, but alarm at happenings in Europe constrained her to develop a new and stronger defence policy in support of her neutrality. She increased her land, sea and air forces together with her not inconsiderable armaments-manufacturing capacity, intimating that she would, if necessary, defend her neutrality against any aggressor. The decline of the League of Nations and of the theory of collective security after the Italian conquest of Abyssinia brought the nations of Scandinavia to consider their position at a meeting in Copenhagen in July 1938. Some kind of a 'Northern' defence pact was discussed, but came to nothing, the weakness and exposure of Denmark being a factor that could neither be overlooked nor overcome.

In 1939 Nazi Germany made an offer to Sweden of a 'non-aggression pact', which, in Nazi terms, meant something only just short of formally joining the Axis, certainly implying and expecting a large degree of sympathy and support. Sweden refused, determined on her neutral course, and stepped up her defence expenditure. Her position was difficult and precarious. To the East, the Russians had designs on Finland, and Sweden could not be indifferent to German and Russian threats to Poland and the Baltic states. To the West, Hitler's Reich depended to some degree on Swedish iron ore and both German and British eyes were on the sea route by which much of the ore travelled down the Norwegian coast towards German ports.

By 1940 her worst forebodings came true and the neutral states on either side of her had been attacked and conquered. To have tried to come to the aid of either Finland or Norway would have been both futile and suicidal, and Sweden could do little but hold grimly to her own neutrality. When the Germans violated this with a demand for transit rights for troops they were at the height of their power and Sweden had little alternative but to give reluctant acquiescence. (Great Britain, Germany's only substantial opponent at the time, fully understood the Swedish position and helped to preserve and encourage what was left of Swedish neutrality.) Sweden resolutely refused, however, to accept Hitler's 'invitation' to join his European 'New Order' in spite of the physical difficulty of trading with anyone except Germany. After the German attack on Russia, Sweden was totally hemmed in by Nazi-controlled territory, since her Eastern neighbour, Finland, joined Germany in the hope of recovering the lands lost to Russia in 1939-40.

Swedish adherence to neutrality was rewarded in the end. By 1943 Germany, increasingly under pressure, was no longer in a position to enforce her demands, and Sweden was able to cancel the embarrassing troop transit arrangements without riposte. As Germany weakened, Sweden managed gradually to free herself from the too close involvement with the Nazi regime which she had been physically unable to prevent.

Opinion in the country was probably neutralist throughout the war, never strongly pro-Nazi, certainly never pro-Soviet. She had numerous difficulties with both sides in matters of territorial violations, contraband claims, espionage and so on, but her primary policy of neutrality in the end served her well.

After the war Sweden came in for a good deal of envious criticism in allied circles for her rather ostentatious prosperity and good living, obtained, it was generally believed, by battening on the combatants while the rest of Europe froze and starved. Sweden, however, took a full and generous part in post-war relief work to less fortunate nations and was an early and active member of the United Nations.

Sweden soon had new problems in foreign policy, having maintained her neutrality successfully, if not exactly triumphantly, through two world wars, both of which had reached her very doorstep. She had suffered neither invasion nor occupation. If she changed her policy now from fear of Russia, most Swedes thought she would be placing herself in the forefront of a contest which would stem from power struggles over which she had no control. Thus, if she joined NATO, she could become merely one of the various battlefields on which the two alien giants might conduct their private and bloody quarrel. She would also acquire new enemies and prejudice old friendships. Swedes realised that they had geography as well as their own defence precautions to thank for their comparative immunity from war in the twentieth century. In the two world wars Germany had nothing to gain either strategically or economically from attacking Sweden. There was really no alternative outlet for Swedish trade, and especially for the vital export of iron ore, which were Berlin's main interests.

In a future war between NATO and the Warsaw Pact, however, circumstances might be very different and Swedish territory could have a high strategic value which would endanger her neutrality. Either side might plan to use Sweden, possibly as a corridor through which to attack on the Northern flank or, equally possibly, to pre-empt defence against such an attack. In either case Sweden would face either blackmail to grant facilities or the prospect of invasion and occupation. These fates have not been unknown in the history of neutral countries standing between warlike opponents, and the pressure or temptation to join one of the alliances is obvious.

From history, self-interest and national sentiment, Sweden has no urge to join the Eastern bloc and such a possibility probably never entered the debate. As to joining the Atlantic

Alliance, some controversy did arise. If she joined, she would have powerful foreign forces to fight alongside her own in case of attack. She would have the guarantee of mutual effort and planning in defence, and the ultimate 'protection', for what it is worth, of the American nuclear deterrent in common with the rest of Western Europe. This, it was argued by some, would better serve to deter Russia than reliance on neutrality and Sweden's relatively small forces. The presence of allied forces and membership of the Alliance would mean that an attack on Sweden was an attack on all NATO. It obviated the risk that Russia might, for strategic reasons, pick a quarrel with neutral Sweden and try to impose 'Finlandisation' or worse.

Arguments for joining the Atlantic Alliance were quite strong, but have been overborne by a substantial concensus. Swedish defence experts believe that, if Sweden assigned her forces to NATO and harboured foreign forces to assist her defence, it would enormously raise tension in Northern Europe. Russia would almost certainly insist on the need for more protection on her Northern flank, justified by its immense naval significance in Soviet planning.

This protection would be only too likely to take the form of a build-up of pressure on Finland for a closer Russo-Finnish defence relationship on the grounds of the NATO threat in the North. The relatively relaxed atmosphere in Scandinavia, the tentative approaches towards disarmament and nuclear-free zones, Sweden's image in the van of peace-seeking nations, would collapse, to be replaced by the leapfrogging of armaments and the frictions of accommodating foreign troops. If Finland, however reluctantly, agreed to draw closer to the Warsaw Pact, there would soon be a confrontation zone on the long Swedish/Finnish border, and both the immediate and the potential threat to Sweden would increase alarmingly, far exceeding the risks inherent in neutrality in an exposed geographical situation. As a result, all sections of responsible Swedish political opinion came down heavily on the side of continued neutrality, and few Swedes regret the decision, although there are serious worries about the cost of the modern weapons which are needed to make neutrality continue to be credible and effective. Swedish neutrality and independence are not cheap. Sweden spends more per head of population on defence than any European NATO member except Britain. She has, luckily, a high income per head from which to pay.

In the event, Swedish neutrality has proved beneficial to the West and to the world. It has reduced tension in Northern Europe, has encouraged Russia to be relatively relaxed in her dealings with Finland, and has so far kept Scandinavia free from the main currents of hostility between the super-powers.

Sweden's system of 'total defence' means what it says, that every able-bodied person is engaged in some capacity in the defence of the country. The Swedish *Defence Manual* states confidently that 'the Swedish Defence Forces are trained and equipped to defend the country against the mechanised forces of the super-powers'. This is not a claim that an attack from any quarter can be defeated, but it is a firm statement of the strategy of 'dissuasion', the demonstration in peacetime that an attack on Sweden might cost even a super-power more than the benefits that could accrue from it.

The numbers of Swedish forces and the volume of her equipment may be small compared to what might be brought against her, but the quality of all is high and the available resources are deployed with skill to make the best use of the very considerable defensive advantages of the Swedish coastline and terrain. In spite of the strategy of 'blitzkrieg attack' prevalent in Soviet military thinking, modern weapons are bringing new hopes and ideas to the defence, and Sweden has been among the pioneers in the field.

Sweden's past military renown and the probable, although untried, prowess and determination of her armed forces, have made Sweden's neutrality credible and widely respected. In spite of some qualms about the expense of modernising her forces, the continuation of the policy of armed neutrality is not in doubt.

Sweden's neutralism is an object lesson in the doctrine that successful neutrality is strong neutrality. The policy has survived two dangerous wars in this century and could survive a third. Better still, it has contributed towards its prevention. Swedish neutrality, and the foreign policy which has stemmed from it, has earned high regard and respect throughout the world. Its violation would bring an aggressor world-wide opprobium.

The neutrality of *Belgium*, now discarded, has a more sombre history. Belgium was made independent of the Kingdom of Holland by the Treaty of 1839, signed by five of the Great Powers of Europe and famous as the 'scrap of paper', for which, according to the sneer of the German Chancellor, Great Britain went to war in 1914. By this Treaty Belgium bound herself to neutrality and was guaranteed in that policy by all the signatories, including Germany. By these guarantees British diplomacy had sought to ensure the paramount British interest that the coast and harbours of the Low Countries of Holland and Belgium should not fall under the sway of either France or Prussia, an anxiety which had often been acute in England when the Netherlands were a Habsburg domain.

In the Franco-Prussian War of 1870, both contestants observed their obligations towards Belgium. Neither Bismarck nor the 1870 von Moltke would have risked bringing Britain into the struggle even had they wished to take the Belgian road to Paris.

Not so in 1914. The so-called 'Schlieffen Plan', the strategy of attacking France through neutral Belgium, was modified and adopted by the 1914 von Moltke. The essence of the plan was speed, to encircle Paris and knock France out of the war before turning on Russia, and an important feature was von Moltke's contemptuous comment that 'we can count on the somewhat inefficient Belgian forces being quickly scattered'. This happened, and 'neutral' Belgium suffered under the German occupation all through four years of war.

The Treaty of Versailles abrogated the 'neutralisation' Treaty of 1839 and Belgium, free to take her own decisions, put her faith in the collective security system of the League of Nations, reinforced by an alliance with Britain and France. By the Locarno agreement of 1925 Germany and Italy joined in guaranteeing Belgium's frontiers, but Belgium then also undertook certain obligations.

With the collapse of the collective security system of the League of Nations in 1936-7, Belgium, with the assent of the other signatories, withdrew from her obligations under the Locarno agreement and reasserted her neutrality, which was accepted and guaranteed by Britain, France and Germany. In the years 1938-40 Belgium made an effort to build defences to a strength compatible with effective neutrality, but the time was too short. Hitler's generals unerringly chose her weak spot in the Ardennes, which the Belgians had thought unsuitable for tank warfare, expecting that, if the Germans came, they would attack on the flat as in 1914. Belgium had to undergo an even more cruel and arduous occupation than in the Kaiser's war.

Belgian experience in this century has been horrifying, but it must be remembered that neutrality served her well for a hundred years. That it failed twice was at least partly because her preparations were inadequate.

Austria has borders with two NATO countries, West Germany and Italy, two Warsaw Pact countries, Czechoslovakia and Hungary, and three non-aligned, Yugoslavia, Switzerland and Liechtenstein.

After the fall of the Habsburg Empire in 1918, the rump of Austria, for centuries one of the great powers of Europe, became a small territory with few resources, huddled round a grossly overgrown capital city. Many Austrians saw the prohibition of joining with Germany imposed on them by the victors of 1918 as being the prohibition of Austria's only real hope of viability. These Austrians were working for an *Anschluss* with Germany long before Hitler seriously considered it. Austria after Versailles was an unhappy, divided country, unsure of itself and its destiny.

After defeat in 1945, and a period of four-power occupation, a policy of neutrality was agreed and this was imposed and guaranteed by the State Treaty of 1955, by which the four occupying powers gave up their 'rights' over this part of the Germany they had defeated. Austria, however, justifiably emphasises that, as a free, independent and democratic republic, she has herself voluntarily declared her neutrality permanent. There are restrictions imposed in the State Treaty on Austria's armed forces and their equipment, but modern Austria accepts, and is proud of, her neutral status. The concept of standing alone, without pledged allies in a dangerous world, has had a strong influence in the development of a cohesive, patriotic and successful nation which was never achieved between the wars nor, for that matter, in the days of Austrian 'greatness'. The new Austria, like her neighbour Switzerland, bids fair to become an island of stability in the middle of Europe.

The Russians did not give this away for nothing, and it is to their considerable advantage that neutral Austria effectively divides NATO's centre from its Southern flank, since movements of foreign troops and military material are, by the State Treaty, not allowed across Austrian territory in peace or war.

Austria, like other neutrals, believes that threats to her security are unlikely to come from an aggressor solely determined to conquer and occupy her territory. They are more likely to arise from the desire to use her as a 'passageway of strategic value' in the context of some wider external conflict. Austrian defence strategy, like that of other neutrals, is based on the concept of 'dissuasion', to ensure that entry into and occupation of her territory can only be achieved, even by a strong military power, at considerable cost. She aims, therefore, to be able to deploy the maximum of resistance by her 'Comprehensive National Defence', which includes the whole population in 'psychological, civil, economic and military' resistance. It is important in a 'dissuasion' policy that not only is it capable of being effective, but that it can be seen to be so. Austria believes that all and sundry must be convinced that Austrian resistance to an aggressor will be fierce and sustained under all the four headings of Comprehensive National Defence.

It seems that the Austrian armed forces are justified in their belief that the State Treaty clauses which restrict their armaments need now to be eased. Austria's stance is entirely defensive and there is no thought of her forces operating outside Austria, so that the existing prohibition of almost all modern weapons should, in fairness, be adjusted to take account of developments since 1955. Without some modern weaponry Austria's 'dissuasion' posture, however sincerely intended, is something of a paper tiger. Her defence expenditure is well below that of other neutrals, whether taken per head of population or as a proportion of GDP. This, combined with the fact of being equipped with hopelessly obsolete weapons, must eventually have a serious effect on the morale of the armed forces.

Finland fought bravely against the Soviet attack in 1939, but was defeated and had to cede the territory demanded by

Russia. She joined with Germany in 1942 to try to recover her losses, again suffering defeat. In the two defeats she was never wholly occupied by Russia and has managed to retain her independence, although with limitations on her armed forces and freedom of military action.

'Finlandisation' is a term too often used in a derogatory sense in the West. Hawkish politicians invest it with a meaning of total dependence on and subservience to the Soviet Union, with a complete submission of national will.

This is totally inaccurate. Although the Treaty of 1948, imposed by the Soviet Union, does restrict Finland's actions in certain cases, and binds her never again to allow her territory to be used as a springboard for attack on Russia, in other fields Finland's relations with her neighbour are of genuine value on both sides. Finland's general orientation internationally is of neutrality, and, if she has to lean to the East in some aspects of defence, she is much closer to Western thought in matters of culture and politics. In trade she maintains an even balance, although she is dependent on Russia for imports of oil. Her attitudes are fully accepted by the Soviets, who perhaps find it convenient to be able to cite Finland as an example of Russian willingness to have co-operative relations with a capitalist state. The Finns cling fiercely to their real political independence and their complex, but fully democratic, constitution. They often criticise and contradict the Soviets, incurring thereby only mild displeasure. When, not long ago, the election was held for a President to replace the aged Dr Kekonnen who had, in his own words, been 'punting upstream' for so many years, the 'Soviet preferred' candidate received a very small proportion of votes and was eliminated in the first ballot. Russia found no difficulty in accepting, and even welcoming, the successful, democratically elected, choice of the Finnish people. The Stalinist, or pro-Russian, Communist Party in Finland has polled very poorly indeed at all the recent elections. A rival, Euro-Communist Party has fared no better.

So 'Finlandisation' is not a merely negative concept. It is a realistic acceptance of historical, geographical and strategic facts by a small state having a 100-mile border with a super-power. It has been a formula for survival in which the essentials of Finland's national independence, neutrality and democracy have been preserved. Finland is the only part of the old Czarist Empire to have achieved and maintained its freedom from the Czar's successors.

Among neutral states *Yugoslavia* is notable in that it has had practical experience of the kind of total warfare on popular and guerilla lines which is the final phase envisaged in the defence strategies of neutral countries whose policies are based on 'dissuasion'. Since neutral states are always weaker than their potential aggressors, and cannot expect quick or total victory, nor threaten retribution, the threat of popular and widespread guerilla-type warfare is a potent factor in 'dissuasion'.

When Marshal Tito, refusing to have his country dominated from outside, broke with Moscow in 1948, the Soviet Government challenged and threatened his position, but Yugoslavs of all races rallied to their great wartime leader and gave him full support. He modified Yugoslav communism significantly away from the Russian model. Since then, Yugoslavia, while improving relations with Russia, has most jealously guarded her independence of Moscow. She has accepted aid and loans from the West and from the East without military commitment to either side. Her freedom from the East was asserted, for instance, when she gave refuge to Hungarians fleeing from the terror of Soviet invasion in 1956.

Yugoslavia is acutely conscious that her position, sandwiched between the two power blocs, has some strategic significance for both. She has frontiers with three Warsaw Pact countries (Bulgaria, Hungary and Romania), two NATO members (Italy and Greece) and two non-aligned (Albania and Austria). She manages to preserve reasonably good relations with all, except perhaps Albania.

The Yugoslav system of 'total' national defence is akin to that of other neutrals we have looked at, but it perhaps permeates the life of the country even more pervasively. Everyone plays his or her part, and many military or resistance organisations are based on factories, villages or other small units. The wartime spirit of the great Tito lives on, and conscription and military training are accepted with pride and enthusiasm. In the event of attack a 'Tito-like' campaign can be activated immediately if the regular forces fail to stem the tide of invasion. Stores of military material are hidden, especially in mountain regions, to ensure that this is no idle threat. Yugoslav 'dissuasion' is designed to make clear to a potential aggressor that the price of invasion would be a long and difficult campaign against trained and competent guerilla fighters. An occupation force would be hampered by civil disobedience and non-cooperation and harassed by guerilla operations. Any strategic advantage hoped for from the attack would be rendered wildly non-cost-effective.

Yugoslavia, through her make-up as a federation of diverse elements, looks the most vulnerable to Russia of the European neutrals. Some of the races maintain their traditional and apparently endemic hostilities. There are minorities with affiliations across the national borders whose loyalty might be questionable under strain. In a deviant communist state, the possibility of revolt by Russian-backed 'orthodox' communists led by ambitious dissidents cannot be altogether discounted. Such a rising, fomented and nurtured by the USSR, might be co-ordinated with an armed incursion from outside in which, as was the case with Czechoslovakia, there would be token support from other Warsaw Pact countries.

These are, mercifully, very much 'worst-case' speculations. Nearly all Yugoslavs value and are proud of their non-aligned status and are conscious and wary of the dangers around them. Yugoslavia has gained admiration and influence throughout the world by achieving and preserving her independence from the Eastern bloc.

This chapter has not aspired to be a complete analysis of the wide and complex range of matters past and presently germane to the concept of neutrality. It has been principally intended to show that the stance is an acceptable, dignified and useful orientation for an advanced industrial country.

Neutral countries have been no les stable, prosperous and happy than those which have pursued the path of alliance. The contributions they have made to the moral strength of the world have been outstanding. The trust and regard in which many of them are held is very great. Strong and reliable additions to their number could be an outstanding contribution to the stability of the world.

Arguments against the status of neutrality have often been vociferous and after each of the world wars the death of the concept was confidently announced.

After the 1914-18 war it was widely believed that the rape of neutral Belgium and the contempt shown by the German submarine campaign for the neutralist United States had proved that neutrality was no longer a viable option. Also it seemed that the new League of Nations, with its collective-security system, might make neutrality superfluous and even dangerous. Neutral countries would not fight unless they were attacked, so the League would be denied the support of neutrals against an aggressor.

After the Second World War the anti-neutralist view has been revived by pointing to the attacks on neutral Belgium, Holland, Norway, Denmark, Yugoslavia and Greece by Germany, and on the United States and China by Japan.

These countries, however, were all weakly armed and almost totally unprepared at the time of the attacks. Those in Europe had not completed any active defence programmes after the collapse of collective security and the League of Nations. Outside Europe, the United States had believed for a century and a half that moral attitudes, distance, the Pax Britannica and the Monroe Doctrine made up a sufficient defence policy.

All countries in situations of any vulnerability now realise that effective neutrality needs arms, but to deduce the death of neutrality from the failures of unarmed neutrals would be grossly misleading. Neutrality is alive and well and, in its most advanced form, living in Europe.

The lesson which has been learned by neutralists in our time is the absolute necessity of backing up the stance with real strength. Adequate defence preparations and high national spirit are a *sine qua non* in the effort needed to create a credible atmosphere of 'dissuasion'. A neutral country must be united and determined in the belief that its policy is morally right and practically viable.

These criteria could be fulfilled in Britain. In the following chapters we shall examine why a switch to the foreign policy of military non-alignment by the United Kingdom would be both practicable and advantageous.

8. *British Neutrality and Foreign Policy*

The first principle in international affairs for Britain, as for other countries, is that her policies shall look to the safety and well-being of her peoples. In the words of Lord Palmerston, 'Nations have no friends, only interests.'

So the safety of our islands must be the primary aim of our foreign policy. Wider goals, such as persuading other nations towards the political, economic or social systems we prefer, or of prescribing what we see as desirable standards of personal freedom or human rights, are not within the compass of the Britain of today. We may still pursue such goals discreetly by example and precept. They cannot have first place in our policy, nor, since our pursuit of them is secondary, should they affect our primary and vital pursuit of security.

A democracy must operate its foreign policy on a consensus basis. If it is to be consistent and successful the general lines of policy, and in particular the orientation on which it is based, must command the support of a substantial majority of the citizens. This has usually applied in Britain where, since the 1939-45 war, it has been the habit of most people and all sizeable political parties to support the alliance stance. There is, however, an increasing volume of opinion, manifested particularly in the debate about nuclear weapons, that somewhere there is a hitch and that there are aspects of foreign policy which are too important to be left to politicians and generals. This has led to more thought and discussion of the principles involved, together with a realisation that the nation's attitude to the foreign environment has a deep influence on the national life which permeates through to every individual.

Analysis and criticism of foreign policy is therefore within the scope of every citizen in a democracy. In exercising this right, the first step is to be sure that the main aims or goals are the right ones, that they are within the power of the nation to achieve, and that the right orientation has been chosen within which they can be pursued.

'Isolation', the deliberate cutting of contact with the rest of the world, is not available as an option to Britain. Our need to import food and raw materials and to pay for them with exports and services makes international commerce an essential. The choice therefore lies between whether we maintain our place in the Western Alliance, in military confrontation with the Warsaw Pact, or whether we switch to the alternative of military non-alignment.

Before we consider the choice in any detail, however, we have to be sure that we have finally discarded our great power spectacles and realised that as a military, industrial and technological nation, Britain is of the second rank. We need also to accept that this change in our circumstances has been fully and accurately reflected by a complete change in the perceptions that other powers have of the United Kingdom.

When Britain was the greatest world power, she was acutely conscious that other nations were always on watch for the opportunity to usurp her position, filch her trade and acquire her 'possessions'. She knew that if she were defeated in war and her homeland invaded or occupied, her days of greatness would be over, her Empire would be dismembered, her industries stripped and her markets shared out by her conquerors. In the perspective of those times, there were tempting prizes to be won by a nation which could decisively defeat the British.

By the 1950s all the events which Britain had so dreaded had come to pass, although not through defeat in war. The industrial and technological capacity of the United Kingdom was far outstripped by the United States and Russia during the war and has now been passed by Japan, West Germany and France. Britain's Gross Domestic Product and her military, naval and air potential are less than a quarter of those of the two greatest powers and below those of other nations in the middle grade. There is no overseas empire to plunder, no exclusive trading rights to be shared out.

Accordingly, a predatory power would know that there are no longer any prizes to be won by attacking or defeating

Britain. We are now only an over-populated offshore island with slender resources, hard put to make our way in the world at all. A conqueror would find us much more of a liability than an asset, and it is impossible to imagine that any foreign power would now contemplate an attack on Britain for the sake of any profits which would accrue from the possession of these islands and the resources they hold.

Reflection on these facts reveals that the concepts on which our imperial policy was founded are now completely out of date, although our policy of alliance continues to rest on those same ideas. But, whether we like it or not, the United Kingdon, in itself, is neither a target nor a factor of any real consequence in the calculations of the greatest powers.

It is time that this very significant development was reflected in our thinking about foreign policy.

To make a satisfactory choice between the alternative orientations available, selection of the one better suited to our long-term wellbeing rests on a comparison of the risks inherent in it with the protection provided.

Risks consist of the danger of being involved in a war and, secondly, of the degree of disaster which might follow such involvement. Protection lies in the possibility that the orientation will avoid war altogether and in the extent to which casualties and damage can be mitigated if war is not avoided. Since we now find ourselves in a stance of alliance, it may well be desirable to ask first whether alliances are, in general, themselves conducive to war.

Alliances are nearly always the product of a foreseen possibility of war. They therefore lead directly to the close contemplation of, and preparation for, war. This 'expectancy of war', the underlying idea that there are problems which can and will be solved by violent means, is widely accepted as important in the analysis of the causes of war. Mr Gordon Allport and other social psychologists believe it to be the primary factor, but this cannot be argued here.

Some alliances, at least, make for prudence in the short term because of the need for consultation among allies. In the long term, however, they are a contributory cause of arms races and a possible source of such misunderstandings as that between the Great Powers which led directly to the First World War. Without alliances wars might well be smaller and the total effects less dire but it is unlikely that they would be less frequent.

As a NATO member Britain would be involved in any war which erupted between America and Russia and therefore an estimate of the risk of British involvement in such a war depends on a comparison between the strength of the factors making war likely and the protection afforded by deterrence.

As for the second level of risk, if there *is* a war, the dangers to our country from attack by missile, air and commando raids and from blockade are immense. Protection against these risks in a super-power war is very feeble. So at best the stance of alliance is an 'all or nothing' situation. As long as deterrence works, we're all right. If it fails, even partially, then . . .

How would an orientation of military non-alignment compare with this sombre picture?

Neutral countries, in assessing the risks of their policy, do not expect to be the sole object of attack for the purpose of conquest and occupation, nor to be subjected to full-scale nuclear bombardment. The risks they face lie in such possibilities as demands for transit facilities or military bases, with the implication that a demand, if refused, might be enforced by military means. These considerations would also apply to a neutral Britain.

All neutral and non-aligned nations nowadays look these possibilities squarely in the face. They are only too conscious that great powers do not in emergency consider the declared neutrality of lesser nations as sacrosanct if there are powerful strategic reasons which urge them to commit a violation. We saw in the last chapter something of the arrangements made by major European non-aligned countries to deal with these possibilities.

Having seen the dangers of alliance and considered some of the existing neutrals, we can turn to the risks and protection which would be associated with a policy of military non-alignment for Britain, making a distinction between the circumstances of peacetime and those which might arise in the event of a war or crisis between the super-powers.

Britain occupies a position of strategic significance on the edge of one of the two main oceans of the Northern hemisphere, a position which both super-powers would be well pleased to occupy as a permanent fortress outpost. But it is not a position which is essential for either provided that it is not controlled by the other. In peacetime neither Russia nor the United States would be likely to risk the universal outrage, the condemnation at the United Nations, the economic sanctions and the possible sequel of a Third World War, all of which might follow an attempt to seize, occupy and use for military purposes a neutral Britain. The scenario is outside any reasonable possibility as a political and military option, and the likelihood that such an operation would be essayed in peacetime in the face of the immense difficulties, complications and dangers it would entail is minimal.

In practice the United States would be much more likely to exercise pressure by other than military means for the renewal of facilities, a possibility which will be examined later.

The Soviet Union would be very unlikely to risk an operation of the magnitude required. The strategic advantages to her of a window on the warm Atlantic would be appreciable, but unless it were politically sustainable through a native communist government, the amphibious invasion of a peacetime neutral Britain is not really a credible military option to be mounted from Arctic Russia.

Would the picture be different in the event of a war between the super-powers in which Britain was a declared neutral?

In this case the effects of the moral and practical effects of world disapproval must be disregarded. They would, however regrettably, be ineffective and it must be assumed that the participants would operate their strategies and make their decisions on a coldly practical calculation of the costs and benefits.

In a war of the super-powers, if either succeeded in seizing Britain, the hope of that power of controlling or denying the Atlantic and the Northern Seas would, in theory, be much improved. One can construct scenarios in the 'just possible' class for such an attack. A Westward thrust by NATO from Europe to support an American transatlantic invasion, perhaps, or an amphibious attack mounted by the Soviets from Murmansk. The chances of such operations being wholly successful, not thwarted by home-based resistance and interference from the other super-power, and of the attacker being able to set up and enjoy useful facilities would not be high. The supply of those facilities, the forces to operate them in the face of a hostile population and the vulnerability of the extra lines of communication required would be a heavy drain to set against any benefits obtained.

Prognostications about plans and strategies for a major war are usually based on a first phase of great ferocity. In a second phase, neither side would be likely to have available the resources required for such 'sideshow' operations as the setting up of an improvised base in a hostile country.

On the first level of risk, then, the chances that a neutral Britain would be attacked in a super-power war are low. On the second level, if she *were* so attacked, the objective would be the use of her facilities and the quality of destruction might be lower than that expected in alliance, when she would enter a war as an ally and host to the forces of a main combatant.

In sum, the real total of risk in a stance of neutrality turns out to be less than that in alliance, and the degree of real protection to be greater.

We cannot leave the risk/protection comparison without some mention of the so-called 'nuclear threat'. This bogey is monotonously trotted out as an argument in favour of Britain's 'own' nuclear weapons ('Without our nuclear shield we would be helpless before a nuclear threat') or in justification of NATO membership ('Without the umbrella of the US deterrent we would be helpless before a nuclear threat').

There is no record or even suggestion that such a threat has ever been issued or contemplated, so we are here in a realm of theory, without practical or historical guidance. Nevertheless, it is a fact that the concept of a 'nuclear threat' plays an appreciable, if imprecise, part in public debate and so needs some clarification vis-à-vis the stance of military non-alignment.

Popular use of the expression suggests that nuclear armaments are useful for the positive exercise of power, and that a country without nuclear weapons or nuclear allies could be coerced to carry out the wishes of a nuclear power against its will. A threat need not be crude or explicit. If determination to secure compliance were strong enough, the implied 'nuclear threat' would, it is suggested, be so clear that the terrified victim would abjectly comply with the demands made upon him.

If this reasoning had the slightest foundation, the whole face of international life would have changed years ago. The logical conclusion could only be that those nations which do not possess nuclear weapons live always in the shadow of the 'nuclear threat' and are perpetually in thrall to the nuclear powers. This is manifestly not the case. Non-nuclear nations have often behaved with freedom, even abandon, in defiance of the wishes of nuclear powers. If they have come to any harm thereby, it has not been through nuclear means.

The reality of power in international affairs is difficult to assess or quantify. Power exists, but there is no simple equation that because A is more powerful than B, then B will generally do as A directs. In the world of rapid communications, public diplomacy and international organisations, the ability of greater nations to exercise power over weaker has sharply declined. The Soviet Union would be infinitely more powerful than an independent, neutral Britain, but there is no way that her nuclear arsenal would contribute to the exercise of undue influence here.

It would be wrong to pretend that nuclear armaments are simply dangerous and expensive toys acquired by powerful governments for prestige and competitive reasons, but their value, even as deterrents, is increasingly in question. The general hatred of these weapons by ordinary people is very great, not least in those countries which 'reluctantly' possess them, and the possibility of their existence being actively and publicly used as a threat suggests an uncharted and highly improbable new dimension in international affairs. Mr G.F. Kennan, from long and intimate knowledge of the United States and Soviet Russia at the international level, has commented on this subject that 'Great nations do not behave like that'.[1]

This chapter began with the proposition that the core aim of British foreign policy ought to be the safety and integrity of our home territory and people. It has now been suggested that a change in foreign-policy orientation from alliance to military

[1] *The Nuclear Delusion* by G.F. Kennan (Hamish Hamilton, 1982)

non-alignment would be the best way to achieve that aim and from this two questions present themselves.

First, why has this apparently sensible option been so little canvassed while Britain's circumstances and responsibilities have been changing? Second, are there considerations which can force or persuade Britain to override the common sense plan of changing her policy to match her circumstances?

One answer to the first question is that our statespersons, military chiefs, media experts and even academics find it distasteful to accept a relatively minor role for Britain in a world dominated by the super-powers. The desire to continue to cut a dash in the great world has led to the refusal to analyse our true status on the international scene.

Because of the characteristic 'openness' of the US governmental method, much of the information required for discussion of American policy is generally available. British public figures and commentators are thereby enabled to take part in a continuing debate, but whether the volume of advice thus engendered has much effect in Washington is a matter of some doubt. It does, however, have an immense effect on the vanity of the politicians and commentators involved, who can convey the impression that some influence in, and leadership of, the Western Alliance lies in their hands.

In discussion in Britain of major foreign-policy issues, the ubiquitous pronoun 'we' seldom refers to the United Kingdom, nearly always to the Western Alliance. British speakers and writers are continually found to be urging that '"we" must talk to the Russians from strength' or '"we" must match the extension of Russian militarism' or '"we" must have the means to deter Soviet expansionism' and so on, all propositions totally outside British capability. In pontificating about what is in fact American policy, British interests are submerged or forgotten. One result has been that neutralism has become a dirty word and the concept of neutrality has been pushed into the background as unworthy of the consideration of a once great power.

Turning to the second question, the security and integrity of the nation are rightly the first aims of foreign policy, but in the case of a change of orientation, it must be established that there are no moral or political factors which could inhibit the change, that defence planning can be adequate and that the position and standing of our country in the world are safeguarded.

Plenty of ink has been spilled on the relation between morals and politics since the time when Plato and Aristotle argued their theories in Athens. We, like they, are still confronted with such general questions as whether policy should be guided by moral considerations. Can a policy so guided work in practice? Who is to dictate the moral values to be used? Without addressing ourselves to these weighty principles we must consider the specific issues which will arise for Britain and the British in the ethical field during a transition to military non-alignment.

Are we morally bound to the military support of the American Alliance, standing in the front line of the defence of its Eastern frontier? Are we morally bound to sustain this commitment indefinitely because we undertook it in the 1950s? Since we support the political values of freedom and democracy, and the Soviet Union does not understand these values in the same way as we do, is there a moral obligation to maintain military confrontation with the Soviets? Because other countries which, in general, share our democratic views and values feel threatened by Soviet military power, is there a moral compulsion to ally ourselves militarily with these countries, even if we do not feel the same threat?

These questions all depend on the argument that Russian militarism is, and is intended to be, a direct military threat to the whole free world. From this it follows that all countries which do not wish to embrace the communist creed or submit to Russian imperialism are under a moral obligation to commit their military forces in support of the United States, which acts as the main bastion of the free world and is therefore entitled to the full and unstinted military support of every nation which also desires to remain free. Non-compliance with this attitude is often said to imply that there is no moral difference between the behaviour patterns of the two super-powers.

Very few in Britain actually believe this. The choice we are trying to establish is in no sense a choice between the moral values of the capitalist United States and the moral values of communist Russia. There may be some reservations about too slavish an acceptance of the whole American competitive and materialistic ethos, but the collectivist tyranny in Russia is almost universally rejected. What is at issue is whether British acceptance of and sympathy with much, if not all, that America aspires to entails a moral obligation to give the United States unequivocal military support in its confrontation with Russian communism, irrespective of the fact that Britain does not herself feel a direct threat, either military or political, from Soviet Russia.

A nation's moral obligations, especially in the military sphere in which so much is at stake, can only be based on that nation's own perceptions. The idea of a moral duty to provide military support for America and West Germany derives from the thirty-five years of the Alliance, in which we have acquired the unfortunate habit of looking at the world, and particularly the Soviet Union, through American or German spectacles. Because these countries have become used to our support and now expect it does not in itself mean that we should indefinitely accept their ideas of our duty. We need to have the courage of our own perceptions of what is the direct military threat. If our perception is that the threat we see is better avoided by neutrality than by confrontation, then our moral obligation is first to the safety of our own people and then to any contribution we can make to the lessening of international tensions.

Another side to this 'moral' debate is whether Britain is committed to permanent military support for American policy because the United States saved Britain from defeat by Germany in two world wars. Or because of the generosity of the Marshall Plan. Or because of the historical and cultural background we share.

No one likes to be accused of ingratitude, but foreign policy is about the future not the past, and practical considerations rate more highly than matters of sentiment.

We need not forget that American participation in both wars 'in aid of Britain' was reluctant in the extreme. Those in the United States who would have backed voluntary participation in war against Germany were a very small minority. In the 1914 war President Wilson won the 1916 election on an uncompromising 'peace' programme. Only the German declaration of unrestricted submarine warfare with 'sink on sight' as its motto, and the actual sinking without warning of an American ship in March 1917, brought America into the war on the British side. Even then, the United States was careful to term itself only an 'associated power', not an ally.

In the 1939 war America never 'came to the aid' of Britain at all, in spite of President Roosevelt's desire to help our beleagured island in 1940. America was finally pushed into fighting Germany by the triumphant declaration of war on the United States by Hitler after the Japanese attack on Pearl Harbour.

Practical considerations have always governed American policy and it is right that it should be so. Practical considerations as seen from London must govern British policy: if these point to an orientation of military non-alignment, they will not be overridden by sentiment, however admirable.

Allied to the suggestion that there is some moral compulsion on nations to join in on the 'right' side in wars, hot or cold, is the attitude that neutrality is, in an undefined way, a despicable stance for Britain. Comparisons are drawn with the strong feelings which were engendered by the continued neutrality of Eire in the war against Hitler's Germany. It was then said that only the Royal Navy and the Royal Air Force stood between Eire and the fate of Belgium, Holland, Denmark and Norway. The 'denial' to Britain of the bases which had been in use by the Royal Navy until shortly before the war was the subject of much bitter comment in Britain, although rights to their use had been freely ceded in 1938.

Irish behaviour in that war, and the attitudes of Britain and her allies to that behaviour, aptly illustrates some of the psychological aspects of neutrality. Most Irishmen, however great their historical dislike of Britain, would not have wished Hitler to win his war and conquer Britain. They well realised that that would have meant his suzerainty over, and probably occupation and control of, Ireland. Most Englishmen and their allies felt a deep resentment that Eire refused to join in the war on what, to them, was manifestly the 'right' side. The bright lights that twinkled across the water in Dublin, lit by English coal, and the freedom of the Free State from the irksome restrictions, hardships and dangers of war infuriated

many. Even Americans, with their widespread sympathy for
the Irish grievances against England, were upset by losses of
ships and men which they saw as avoidable had Eire been
willing to co-operate.

Superficially the case against the morality of Irish neutrality
when the chips were down in that war is powerful. The 'free
ride' argument, that Eire could not and would not have
survived as a free and independent country had Britain gone
under, is strong, and the Irish Government and people knew
this perfectly well.

There is, however, another side to the coin. The Irish had no
part in the Anglo-French relations with Germany which
preceded the war. They would not have been listened to if they
had. To say that there was a moral compulsion on Eire to join
the Allies because their cause was 'right' is a statement with
very far-reaching implications. It can be read to mean that
every nation is 'morally bound' to make a decision in black
and white on the rights and wrongs of all serious international
disputes and divisions, the grey, common in such matters,
being inadmissible. Having made this decision, the nation
then would apparently be 'morally bound' to throw its
military weight into the scale on the side it had deemed to be
'right'. Manifestly, international relations are not conducted
like that and never will be. Lesser nations as well as greater
conduct their affairs according to how they see the interests of
their peoples, not according to moral considerations selected
by others. It is totally unacceptable that the greatest powers
alone shall decide the issues of war and peace on behalf of a
multitude of smaller nations.

The 'morality' of neutrality cannot be measured by the
degree of resentment directed against neutrals by belligerents
either in war or in cold war. Those actively involved in a
military sense are not unnaturally obsessed with the rectitude
of their cause and the superiority of their method. They
believe that all who favour their cause should join them. That
way there are no bounds set to belligerence, and this can be in
no one's interest.

There is a moral element in foreign policy, but it cannot be
divided into the simple choice between black and white,
goodies and baddies. All depends on the circumstances of a
nation, on its perceptions of safety and threat, of good and ill

will, of risk and protection. No nation has the right to dictate its own perceptions to another, nor to prescribe moral imperatives based on those perceptions.

There is now no possible moral compulsion for Britain to take part in the defence of West Germany, nor to involve herself militarily either in the tangled affairs of Central Europe or in the strained relations of the super-powers. There is no moral standard which dictates that we should demonstrate our willingness to take part in a war in which we have no direct interest and in which we, probably more than any other participant, risk destruction. If we believe the values of democracy to be preferable to the values of the communist bloc, and it is pretty clear that we do, our contribution can still be better made by the independent and peaceful dissemination of those values, a role for which we are perhaps uniquely qualified.

It cannot be made too clear that there are no political overtones in the suggested change of orientation to neutrality. Neutralism is no cloak for communist sympathies. Sweden and Switzerland are not exactly teetering on the brink of communism, nor do Austria or even Yugoslavia show much sign of throwing themselves into the Soviet camp.

Neutral Britain would not want any 'special relationship' with the communist bloc, nor wish to act in any way as 'go-between'. She would seek no more than the most cautious and correct relationship with the Soviets and expect the same in return. Independence would probably make British attitudes to communism and to the prickly and suspicious regime in the Kremlin more wary than it now is. Russia as she has been governed for the last thousand years, whether by Tsars, boyars or commissars, has little affinity with Britain, the original home of political freedom.

Military non-alignment in Britain would not promote or encourage Russian and communist expansionism. What encourages communism and invites Russian interventionism is disorder, chaos, internal strife, discontent, repression, violence, extortionism, great luxury contrasting with utter poverty, bribery, crime and corruption, seething shanty-towns. These form the seed beds in which communism best festers and grows and it is where these evils are not attacked by the West that the specious communist cure-all remedies sound most attractive to an audience without hope. The well-armed, well-prepared neutral, standing aside from the military confrontation of the super-powers, does more to fight communism, totalitarianism and the trampling on human rights than all the sabre rattling and provocation of the arms race. Neutrality can stand up with confidence to any political criticism, either internally or from our erstwhile allies.

If Britain moves out of the Western military Alliance she must move into real independence, not into a position in which she could be vulnerable to threat or attack. For defence here and not on the Elbe, she will, like other neutrals, have to indicate to the world that she will not let attack or blackmail succeed. We have seen 'dissuasion' practised by much weaker neutrals than ourselves, in more exposed situations and with fewer resources and defensive advantages than we have in these islands. These countries believe that their stance, and the strength and determination they bring to it, is enough to dissuade any country from either attacking them or making a demand for their facilities.

None of this is sure, but in an uncertain world no security is absolute. In a dangerous time it is only possible to try to select the best course available.

The defensive strategy known as 'dissuasion' has become part and parcel of an effective foreign policy orientation of military non-alignment. In the next chapter we turn to see how this concept can be applied and adapted to the problems and capacity of a neutral Britain.

9. *British Neutrality and Defence*

Neutrality is often derided by ill-wishers as entailing pure pacificism, conscientious objection to the bearing of arms or total unilateral disarmament. In the modern world neutrality means none of these things. It is essentially a hard-headed and practical policy which entails defence preparations on a considerable scale, needing the support and co-operation of the whole nation.

In Chapter 7 I indicated how the armed neutrals of Europe effect national security. A neutral Britain, with her island geography, her wide technological base, her large population, her military, air and naval traditions, her sizeable arms industry and her highly trained and well-equipped regular forces, could implement a policy of 'dissuasion' as effectively as any of the smaller neutrals.

In Chapter 6 there was set out the pattern of deployment of the British armed forces as it is now, based on the primary task of defending the West German frontier against attack from the East. With a change in orientation, the task would change to that of setting up in Britain itself a defence adequate to dissuade an aggressor from making an attack. The new task is clearly very different from the old, but it would have to be undertaken by the forces in existence at the time of the changeover. The difficulties and inefficiencies inevitable in trying to perform the second task with the budget, equipment and personnel which have been for thirty-five years geared to the first, should not be underrated. They will be formidable indeed, but not insurmountable.

With the return to Britain of the British Army of the Rhine and the 2nd Tactical Air Force there will, for the first time since the last war, be an effective core around which a genuine defence of Britain can be built. Although these are two of the finest and best-trained fighting forces in the world, neither is ideally equipped or specifically trained for the role of home defence. Nevertheless, with the help of the skeleton already in existence, they will rapidly form the basis of a proper island defence. The expense of their repatriation will not be small and, although savings in transport and other expense connected with their maintenance abroad will soon show through, these will be more than absorbed for some time by the provision of more accommodation and facilities in Britain.

The withdrawal of staff officers and support from the various NATO Headquarters would release experienced officers for the replanning of home defence and the extensive reorganisation and administrative problems involved. Some existing weapons and vehicles will be unsuited for the new tasks, and there will be a good deal of 'making do' at first while a different emphasis in mobility and fighting technique is planned and implemented. None of this will be easy, nor particularly agreeable for servicemen rather pleasantly 'dug in' to their present life. The whole of the 55,000 men of BAOR, however, and all the twelve squadrons of 2nd TAF who are presently occupied in the defence of West Germany will be fully employed in setting up the organisation for the defence of Britain on its own shores.

The second of the functional divisions of the British armed forces in the present orientation of alliance is the Royal Navy, whose role in the defence of neutral Britain would have to change just as traumatically.

As we saw in Chapter 6, of the main fleet of some sixty odd 'major' surface fighting vessels and twenty-seven 'attack' submarines, much the larger part is allocated to NATO in peacetime and nearly the whole would be so employed in war. The main role is the defence of the American reinforcement routes in the Eastern Atlantic and the approaches to Europe, which includes assistance in containment of the Soviet fleet and submarines based at Murmansk. This fairly wide-ranging semi-ocean role, carried out in association with the United States and the other NATO allies, gives British naval forces a window on global strategy at sea which has been a part of the British naval outlook for four hundred years.

Little of this would be of value in the 'dissuasion' strategy for the defence of neutral Britain, which would entail some withdrawal into home waters and an intensification of reconnaissance, inshore and anti-submarine activities.

The primary task of the Royal Navy on relinquishing its NATO role would be to assure, without help from outside, the naval defence of our island. This would at first have to be undertaken by a fleet which is neither designed nor suitable for the task, and which lacks much of the equipment desirable. It is, however, a fleet of considerable size and power which would no doubt adapt itself with skill and ingenuity to the new circumstances.

The third arm of our NATO-orientated defence forces is the controversial strategic nuclear deterrent force, consisting of four 'Resolution' class submarines, each armed with sixteen 'Polaris' missiles. The 'Chevaline' modification now being installed will upgrade each missile to carry six warheads. This force is operated by the Royal Navy but takes no part in normal naval duties and is rightly tabulated as a separate functional entity. We have immediately to consider whether Britain, as a non-aligned power, would need or wish to retain her 'independent' nuclear deterrent, and whether she would be able to do so.

Arguments in favour of a neutral Britain keeping a strategic nuclear deterrent in her defensive armoury have to be culled from the mainstream of nuclear controversy. Five arguments can be put forward:

(1) Deterrence, the threat of reprisal by nuclear means against any power that attacks us, and the hope that superior nuclear powers would not make nuclear threats or attacks for fear of provoking a nuclear response

(2) The prestige, such as it is, of belonging to the 'nuclear club'

(3) The value of such weapons as a bargaining counter in disarmament or arms control negotiations

(4) The value of 'theatre' and 'tactical' nuclear weapons as a cheap war-fighting option

(5) The possession of nuclear weapons as insurance against proliferation.

Each of these arguments requires serious consideration.

It has already been suggested that the theory of deterrence has become so confused as to be losing its credibility. To rely on nuclear weapons to deter attack by a non-nuclear power is unnecessary when defence can be reasonably well assured by modern conventional means. For a lesser nuclear power to consider or threaten a nuclear exchange with a greater power would be nothing less than national suicide. The shadowy concept of a 'nuclear threat' was rejected as a practical possibility in the last chapter. Unless we accept the serious credibility of such threats, maintaining a counter-threat against them is wasteful, if not absurd.

One leg of the 'prestige' argument is that the retention of a substantial nuclear potential has, to some extent, masked Britain's decline, and that to abandon this symbol of power and competence in technology would be to admit the collapse of all pretensions in international status. In particular, and this might be especially hard to bear, it would leave France triumphantly more powerful than Britain in Europe. The ghosts of Napoleon and General de Gaulle would be dancing together in Valhalla.

This view can possibly be countered by the opposite argument that the renunciation of strategic nuclear weapons is a moral gesture of at least some significance and that the French *force de frappe*, already the only nuclear force in the West independent of the super-powers, is in fact an exercise in considerable futility, having no real defensive rationale to show for great expense and effort. For neutral Britain to maintain a wasteful competition of this sort for a non-existent prize would be the height of folly.

The 'top table', or bargaining counter, argument can still be heard occasionally, although its tones are fainter than they were. It becomes clearer that the 'top table' is the 'top table' and, as such, will always be occupied only by the greatest powers, even if they allow some of the 'children' in sometimes for a treat. The conclusion must be that what power and influence can be gained from the possession of nuclear weapons is little use to Britain now, and would be of even less in a neutral stance.

The 'multilateralist' argument, that by hanging on to our nuclear weapons Britain will be better able to persuade others to renounce or reduce them in equal negotiation, cannot now be used with much confidence. The scale of the arsenals of the super-powers, each of whose strategic weapons run into four figures, hardly makes Britain's four submarines, even when updated into 'Trident', very impressive bargaining counters.

The 'cheap war fighting' argument does not apply to Britain's present strategic equipment, which is only accurate enough to attack urban or area targets. Even if Britain does not opt for neutrality before we are equipped with the much more accurate and powerful 'Trident', there is no place in Britain's plans for 'dissuasion' for the kind of war fighting supposed to be contemplated between accurate first-strike and counter-force strategic nuclear weapons. This is not a vocabulary which even the most powerful country would use in relation to its own forces.

The last argument, about the danger of the proliferation of nuclear weapons, is more difficult to assess. Everyone must fear these weapons being in the hands of irresponsible rulers or of isolated nations in desperate straits. There are those who honestly believe that the abandonment of nuclear weapons by a prominent nation would be a potent example, but it has to be admitted that example has seldom proved an effective force for good in international life. As in other spheres, a bad example seems easier to follow than a good, and whether the retention or abandonment by Britain of her strategic nuclear force would have any effect on proliferation must remain a matter of opinion. If, however, proliferation should suddenly become widespread, there is no denying that a Britain without nuclear weapons might begin to feel distinctly uncomfortable, if not, as Aneurin Bevan put it, 'naked'.

None of the arguments for retention is by itself particularly compelling and even taken together they hardly make a strong case. The clinching factor might be that a United States Congress would probably be unwilling (and might be legally unable) to continue the supply and servicing of secret and vital parts of the 'Trident' missile to a nation not within the American-led alliance. To try to substitute a British system would take time, considerable effort and a great deal of money. It probably could be done, but the decisions not to undertake such a project, but to buy from the US first Polaris and then Trident, indicate that, unless an independent strategic deterrent were a necessity for survival, the enterprise would not be worthwhile. Britain has already notched up some horrendous bills for expensive failures and U-turns over the development of high-technology defence equipment.

In sum the balance seems heavily weighted against retention. It is to be hoped that relinquishment can be effected with dignity, after consideration of any new circumstances at the time of British withdrawal from the Alliance.

There is little to be said about the last two sections of our present-day defence. Home defence by air, sea and land is abysmally weak and only too apt to be cannibalised to provide for everything else. Under non-alignment it would be 'top of the pops', a status it has only enjoyed for very short periods when we faced Napoleon and Hitler. What is now in position will, of course, be invaluable as a basis upon which to start building the much bigger organisation which will be needed.

What was called in Chapter 6 the 'residual' commitment would not be excessively affected by the switch to neutrality. Alliance partners and allies have not shown much interest in, nor been disposed to give appreciable help in, Britain's difficulties about these complications left over from the time of empire. There is no reason to have expected that they should. However, the fact of Britain more obviously standing alone might well encourage a more aggressive attitude in those nations which feel grievances and are stating claims against Britain. This should concentrate our mind to try harder to solve problems which cannot be allowed to stand over indefinitely. Meanwhile the 'residual' defence commitment will not go away. In neutrality we should have to be prepared to maintain and even, if necessary, to reinforce it, while working strenuously to find political solutions to the underlying problems for which we cannot abjure our responsibility.

The requirement for defence is continuous and will not admit of any serious hiatus. In considering the defence arrangements for a new foreign-policy orientation, there is, therefore, no alternative to using for the new stance the forces in being for the old. Having taken stock of these forces, we need to ascertain how they can best be used immediately to assert a policy of 'dissuasion'.

The four major European neutrals, Austria, Sweden, Switzerland and Yugoslavia, all have the same underlying philosophy of 'dissuasion' but, because of differences in their geography and circumstances, they differ greatly in organisation, deployment, weaponry and strategic planning. In deciding strategic policy, on which all else depends, it is necessary to define closely what objectives can reasonably be expected to be possible of achievement with the means available. Mere rhetoric will not dissuade anybody. The choices lie along a spectrum ranging from the complete exclusion of an aggressor through the options of destroying him by 'in-depth' defence by regular forces, attrition by regular, territorial and local defence units to the extremes of guerilla and partisan warfare with the ultimate step, after occupation, of civil resistance and sabotage. Some or all of these methods are planned, or at least envisaged, to a greater or less degree by the existing neutrals, but, although Britain will have much to learn from their experience, we shall not be able to model our own planning fully on any one of them.

All four countries operate systems of full conscription of the male population and in Austria, Switzerland and Yugoslavia the concept of the citizen army and territorial defence occupies much of their effort. These countries assert their intention of denying entry by means of regular troops and static fortifications at frontiers, but their realistic planning on a large scale depends more on the use of their citizen armies, relatively lightly armed, mobile troops who would harass, attack and, hopefully, envelop and destroy an invader who had violated their frontiers.

Only Sweden at present intends to pursue the policy of military defence within its own borders by a mobile field army, capable of moving with heavy equipment and fighting in any part of the country with sophisticated, modern weapons. This army, however, expects to be given time to mobilise by the primary defensive efforts of the Navy or Air Force, whose duty it is to stop invasion at the coast or, in combination with the specialised 'Norrland' brigades, along the Finnish border in the North of the country. Because of the ever-mounting expense and complication of weapons and the necessity of maintaining all three arms of defence at high efficiency, it seems that Sweden may have to modify her strategy, although she is understandably reluctant to do so.

British planning for 'dissuasion' would almost certainly be along Swedish Lines, but with emphasis on totally denying entry to the country to an invader or attacker.

In Britain the conviction that we have a natural right to absolute security in our island has built up over the centuries behind the supremacy of the Royal Navy, first the 'wooden walls', then the Grand Fleet. Having been severely dented by the German air raids and invasion threat of 1940-41, that confidence has now returned, fostered, perhaps erroneously, by the illusion that defence on the Elbe will keep war on the continent, well away from Britain. British public opinion would be very unlikely to take kindly to a military strategy which was not aimed at the total denial of entry to our country. As the composition of forces at the changeover time would fit into such a pattern and into no other, there is every reason that it would form the basis of British 'dissuasion' planning.

On this assumption, an island nation needs for its defence a regular Navy and Air Force of high technological standards as the first bastions of defence, with well-armed and mobile forces on land able to deal quickly with any penetration beyond the coast.

The aim of forward defence for an island is that an enemy should be stopped before landing either by sea or from the air. To defend a long coastline with a naval force which may be inferior to the attacker means that the first assault on the invasion force must be as far from land as possible, by air, submarine, missile and mine. If a force were landed, then it becomes the task of the Army and Air Force to destroy that force and of the Navy and Air Force to harass and cut its lines of communication and reinforcement.

The most important part of the tactics of all three services is that they remain in being, able to strike continuously without ever risking their full strength. If it is not practicable against a formidable opponent to obtain command of the sea and air, it is vitally important not to lose it. To effect this entails a high degree of dispersal and concealment, with much delegation of responsibility and great efficiency of equipment and personnel in command, communications and intelligence. The object of the defence is not necessarily to destroy the enemy immediately but to make his invasion attempt abortive.

These considerations indicate the likelihood of new principles and ideas entering the philosophy of the fighting services, probably leading cautiously towards more emphasis on ruggedness, simplicity and survivability and less on excessive reliance on elaborate technology. Numbers, too, will be of the essence, in order that the invader is continually, and ultimately unacceptably, under pressure or attack.

The vigour and determination with which the home defence could be put into effect would depend on the armed services receiving a degree of support from their political masters rather above what has often been their lot in the past. It would be of great importance for the morale of the country and its defenders that the urgency and true value of the task should be very widely appreciated, and that the new structure should be in fighting trim as soon as humanly possible after the decision on the policy of neutrality.

There is little point in trying to indicate here the exact force which would best implement British defence by 'dissuasion'. But it is desirable that it should be demonstrated that the policy is not a pacifist pipedream but a practical option for all three services. The process of conversion to totally suitable equipment and force strengths will be slow, not least because of the expense and complication of modern weapons systems. Even the move indicated towards more simplicity and greater numbers must be qualified by the fact that accurate targeting and guidance systems are the basis of effective defence weapons and the best are unlikely to be cheap or simple.

Taking the *Royal Navy* first, it is likely that there would be no requirement for some time ahead for the provision of major surface vessels, of which there are enough in the existing fleet to look after the defence of home waters, with some allowance for the 'residual' commitment. These ships would have to be employed in some tasks for which they were not designed until smaller and more suitable craft became available. It would not be expected of the navy of a neutral power to be capable of maintaining or winning any kind of fleet action against a greater power in the open seas.

An elaborate system of mine defences is an important part of coastal defence in neutral strategies and Britain would be no exception. She has, indeed, long experience of this form of warfare in the difficult waters around her, but it might be even more important during a war in which we were trying to maintain our neutrality. The present planning would be eligible for early review.

Fast-attack craft, armed with missiles, torpedoes or guns, constitute an arm of sea warfare very important in neutral thinking. It was extensively used by both sides in the 1939-45 war, but, according to the *Military Review 1983-4* of the International Institute for Strategic Studies, it has fallen out of favour in British thinking, since no craft are listed for the Royal Navy. Sweden has thirty-four, Yugoslavia thirty-one, Finland sixteen and even Albania eighteen of these craft and it seems certain that a considerable establishment would be needed to strengthen British coastal defence.

The Royal Navy's anti-submarine warfare capacity would retain or increase its present great importance, although the emphasis would change from the protection of shipping to the denial of British waters to foreign submarines in a war in which Britain was neutral. It would be made clear that the use of British waters by combatant submarines would not be tolerated and would be made extremely hazardous. To neglect this would be the best way to encourage one or both combatants to demand the use of British facilities in order to deny British waters to his opponents. The proximity of Britain to the sea area where direct contact between the super-powers would be fierce and frequent in a war between them, makes this concept very important in a British neutral strategy.

British submarine capacity and experience is very considerable, although now insignifiant in numbers compared to that of either the US or the USSR. Britain is the only country outside the super-powers to operate a substantial fleet of nuclear-powered attack submarines, the efficiency of which was demonstrated in an ocean role in the Falklands war. Although these vessels might seem more powerful than would necessarily be needed by a neutral, their range, capacity to remain at sea and to stay submerged for long periods and ability to hunt enemy submarines would be invaluable, even if their ultimate renewal and replacement might be doubtful. This would also depend on the outcome of the controversy as to whether air, surface or undersea elements prove the most efficient submarine hunters. A neutral Britain would be unwise to make appreciable reductions in her submarine fleet at least for a while.

To suggest that the time has come for the Royal Navy to relinquish once and for all its ocean-going role would be a difficult bullet indeed for the senior service to bite. The shades of Drake, Hawke and Nelson would be invoked and all sorts of improbable contingencies suggested. These great men, however, only asked for the vehicles and armaments appropriate to the work they had in view, and the Admirals of a neutral Britain would ultimately do the same. The 'residual' commitment will in any case keep ocean-going in business for long enough to work out in detail the long-term plan for the Royal Navy.

The three anti-submarine warfare (ASW) aircraft carriers now maintained may seem superfluous, or at least too many, for a neutral country, but it would probably be a mistake to scrap or sell any of them immediately. Their retention would be the clearest demonstration that a neutral Britain has no intention of being a weak Britain, and the image of neutrality in general would benefit wherever they were seen. They would play a big part in the setting up and consolidating of the naval and ASW defence of Britain even if their role hardly stretches into the indefinite future. The part played by the present Fleet Air Arm in anti-submarine warfare is so important that it would be dangerous to suggest any early diminution in the role and size of this branch of the Navy. It would be in a reduction in the numbers of the more powerful ships, the guided-weapon-carrying destroyers and the general purpose frigates that economies would be sought, but the importance of morale and of demonstrating Britain's resolve to maintain strong and fully armed neutrality would preclude any hasty economies until the non-neutral world adopts more peaceful attitudes and makes appropriate arrangements in the fields of arms control and disarmament.

The *Royal Air Force* would be confronted with the immediate task of adapting its existing strength to the sole function of defending the home base and surrounding waters. The return to Britain of the force deployed in the defence of West Germany would supply an appreciable increase in the quality, quantity and coverage of home defence. The two squadrons of interceptors, two of close support and one of reconnaissance aircraft would fit in with the existing pattern and suffice to provide for the initial stage of the air defence of neutral Britain.

A more difficult problem, political as well as military, is the future of the considerable force of strike/attack squadrons of the Royal Air Force. There are some thirteen in all, seven or eight of which are now in Germany. Most of the aircraft can carry nuclear weapons, although the normal load is conventional. The missiles and aircraft are not classified as 'strategic', although they cannot truly be described as 'tactical' or or 'battlefield' weapons.

The question of the holding of the smaller nuclear weapons by a neutral power must be considered later in relation to all three services, since all hold and are prepared to use such weapons. Here we are concerned with whether neutral Britain would need or wish to retain a force of strike/attack squadrons of any kind.

The fact that no other neutral deploys such aircraft is not conclusive since all are lesser powers than Britain, with much smaller populations and resources. They may well eschew these weapons simply because they are unable to afford or produce them.

Britain should not, in the long term, need a force of the size now at her disposal, which for a neutral might well be considered provocative and would, anyway, be wasteful. Strength, however, is the essence of successful neutrality and it would be taking altogether too superficial a view of the international problems of the future to assert that a country of the size and importance of Britain should at once dispose of all capacity to retaliate. France, although a member of the Western Alliance, preserves a fiercely independent view of her own defences and has built up what, for a medium power, is a formidable attack potential of aircraft and missiles in addition to her submarine fleet. Neutral Britain, outside the Alliance, would be able to reduce her strike/attack force on withdrawal from Germany and would reconsider its mission. In this, as in other matters, however, she should proceed with circumspection, not taking irrevocable steps until she has 'felt the water' of neutrality for some time.

For the Royal Air Force, as for the other services, a cardinal principle of 'dissuasion' is that the force remains in being, able to continue attacking the invader and his communications. An essential and difficult technique which will need much development will be the dispersal and concealment of weapons, platforms, aircraft, personnel and maintenance facilities. A defensive force simply cannot afford the risk that a surprise bombardment, effected by very accurate targeting techniques, might destroy its core before it could be used.

In time there would develop an assessment of a balance between the 'bests' of high technology needed to repulse a sophisticated attacker and the larger amounts of more rugged and less elaborate equipment able to survive and continue the attack. The shape of things to come may be guessed from the recent equipment with missiles of a number of training aircraft for home defence. This type of imaginative thinking will play a considerable part in 'dissuasion', but such technological skills as the RAF's pioneering mastery of vertical/short take-off techniques will also be invaluable.

On the assumption that the 'dissuasion' policy of Britain takes the form of planning for the task of frustrating any attack on our country short of the improbable event of full-scale launch of nuclear missiles, the role of the main fighting strength of the *Army* will be very unlike that to which it has become accustomed in defending the Eastern frontier of Germany. There the front is narrow, the avenues of approach are limited and something of the enemy's plans and dispositions can be foreseen. Here no such constants can be assumed. The first problem would be to ensure enough dispersal and concealment to frustrate a heavy first wave of air and missile attack, and to combine this with the ability to muster and bring to bear with great speed the degree of force required to abort landings from either sea or air in any part of the country.

There seems little reason to expect that any immediate and drastic changes in equipment would be required, except for strengthening the numbers of surface-to-air missiles, greater mobility for all arms and increases in the new and smaller hand-held missiles. The combat strength of the Army is unlikely to satisfy the full requirements for total defence of Britain, but the emphasis in the first years of neutrality would be on organisation, construction of static and coastal defence posts, the integration of territorial and reserve units into their mobilisation tasks and the devising of new tactics. There would be a very great deal to be done.

Britain's Army when mobilised would not amount to more than 250,000 first-line troops. Sweden, with a population less than one-sixth of ours, expects to put half a million men in the field within seventy-two hours of alert. The British mentality at present is to say: 'It's all right as long as West Germany is defended. Nothing can happen here', but this won't do if 'dissuasion' is to be effective. There will be a long way to go and it is upon the Army that most responsibility for making up the leeway is going to fall.

The neutral countries of Europe all base their 'dissuasion' policies on a system of universal conscription, showing the ability and intention to call the whole nation to arms in emergency. Without conscription none of them could train in peacetime the personnel they need to perform the tasks laid down in their policies if, against their will, they are involved in war. None could maintain on a full-time basis the armed services that would be necessary even in the early stages for adequate defence. It has already been emphasised in Chapter 6 that no neutral finds that the liability to national service is a burden on its community. On the contrary, it is accepted cheerfully and indeed forms a considerable bond for unity. The part that citizens, all citizens, play in the defence of their country is an appreciable factor in maintaining the will to survive in freedom which is all-important to a convincing stance of 'dissuasion'.

The question naturally arises whether neutral Britain would feel impelled to follow them and adopt universal conscription, breaking a long tradition of voluntary service which has produced strong public distaste for compulsory service in peacetime.

There are arguments on both sides. As with the other neutrals, the job cannot be done in Britain entirely by expensive regular forces. The only efficient method is to enlist and train a considerable auxiliary force available to reinforce the regulars at short notice. But the population of Britain is so large as to make universal conscription unwieldy and inefficient. The organisation, administration and training required would take up far more of the time, skills and resources of the armed forces than can economically be spared. The numbers involved in a yearly call-up could not fail to make serious inroads into the efficiency and readiness for combat of the first lines of defence; worse, the number of conscripts would rapidly become greater than the services would either wish or be able to accept. The temptation would be inevitable in today's highly technical orientation of the services, to put the conscripts on to chores, square bashing or no job at all, with results disastrous to the morale of conscript and regular. There was not a senior soldier, sailor or airman who did not breathe a long sigh of relief when wartime conscription was finally abandoned some fifteen years after the last war. Although it would not be true to say that the job could not be done by conscription in Britain, it is fairly sure that it would not be well done. It could, by undermining confidence and morale, wreck the whole concept of 'dissuasion' and therefore neutrality.

Other countries, notably the United States, have experimented with a selective draft system, but besides being very difficult to administer, this tends to be invidious, leading to complaints of favouritism and privilege, which discredit the system. It is tempting to toy with such ideas as a 100 per cent call-up, with the services taking their needs on a semi-voluntary basis and the civil authority providing occupational training or social work for the remainder. There are obvious objections to such schemes, which anyway present social problems outside the scope of this book.

However, it is clear than an effective 'dissuasion' policy cannot be operated entirely by regular forces, even in Britain. Either larger permanent forces would be maintained than the country could afford or readily assimilate or, if numbers were kept down, defence would fall below the required standard.

The best solution seems to lie in the expansion and upgrading of the Territorial Reserve, Volunteer Reserve and Auxiliary arms of all three services. This must not be, as it has so often been in the past, merely a paper exercise to get some more names on the books. These arms will have to be well-trained, well-equipped, well-exercised and well-paid, ready to take an important place alongisde the regulars at a moment's notice. This will cost money, which must not be grudged out of the savings which will show from the discard of some of the functions now existing in connection with NATO.

Improved recruiting inducements will be required to dispel

the drab image evoked by Territorial service. It must be made attractive to the many people in our time, men and women, who have plenty of leisure, even if it is sometimes involuntary. Tax-free pay is an obvious necessity, longer fully-paid initial training, more fully integrated exercises, more and better equipment and accommodation, use of playing fields, exercises abroad in other neutral countries, there are plenty of possibilities. Above all, the interest, respect and pride of the regulars in drawing closer to, and taking more responsibility for, the second line is vital. A large, efficient and keen Territorial, Reserve and Auxiliary force is not only necessary for 'dissuasion' but will have the effect of bringing the forces closer to the country and the country closer to the forces.

The discarding of the conscription option means that neutral Britain would not use quite the same strategies as other neutrals who seek to fill out their plans to halt an invader at the coast or frontier with the concept of territorial defence in depth, operated by lightly armed forces operating in small units and using local knowledge and favourable terrain to hinder and harass an invader. If this is unsuccessful against a heavily armed invader, as it might well be, there is an implication, not usually very clearly spelled out for understandable reasons, that they will resort to guerilla warfare, and ultimately to partisan and sabotage operations supported by civil disobedience.

British territory is not particularly well-suited to territorial in-depth defence nor to guerilla warfare. Natural obstacles are few, roads and communications good and plentiful. If an invader succeeded in obtaining a foothold substantial enough to start building up the strength needed to subdue and occupy the whole country, in-depth defence would obviously be required, but it would be conducted by regular forces under command. In a country as densely populated as Britain, to resort to irregular and unco-ordinated warfare would expose the population to great hardship and be unlikely to achieve any substantial result. While air and sea forces remain in being, the home defence will be much more sure of ejecting the enemy by well-planned operations than by haphazard harassment. Neutral Britain will be wise not to cultivate a 'last ditch and last man' mentality, but to build and maintain balanced forces in which she can repose complete faith.

The question of the retention of tactical nuclear weapons by all three services will need early and earnest consideration by politicians and defence authority. It cannot be easily wished away by saying that since no other neutral maintains these weapons, neutral Britain should not. There is no direct comparison with the European neutrals, since their small size and limited resources are significant barriers, although Sweden and Switzerland might find small 'nukes' within their capacity if they so wished.

Several questions will need examination. Is it morally unacceptable for a neutral country to deploy tactical nuclear weapons? Would any nuclear weapons be particularly effective in the defence of Britain? Would the retention of tactical nuclear weapons invite the use of nuclear weapons against us? How do we see the future of proliferation? Would we mind if, say, France, Argentina, Israel, South Africa, Iraq and Libya all had nuclear weapons and we hadn't? If we gave them up, would we deliberately ensure that we could not make them again quickly? Would the retention of some nuclear weapons (e.g. anti-ship missiles, depth charges, anti-aircraft missiles) undermine public support for 'dissuasion'? Could any nuclear weapons be used without doing unacceptable damage to ourselves?

These, and others, are hard questions and of the greatest importance, but they have little to do with the essentials of neutrality as the most practical and sensible option for Britain. The issue can well be left for debate when neutrality is achieved. Then the degree of safety or danger which Britain perceives, the defensive utility of the weapons we have and the development of world opinion on nuclear warfare can be better assessed. The answer is likely to be a clear rejection on an objective view of the balance of risk/protection involved, but it is only sensible not to prejudge the issue. Neutrality must be argued on practical political and military grounds, and not on the totally different issues of moral and emotional ideals. All important in the debate is the knowledge that in a stance of neutrality, and probably only in that stance, can we decide these matters for ourselves, as, for instance, Sweden and Switzerland have already done.

The subject of national defence in a country of the size and industrial capacity of Britain is inevitably intimately connected with its defence industry and the procurement of the weapons it requires.

Proposals for British neutrality entail a drastic change in our military alignment, but there is no intention that the change will lead to any drastic differences in our commercial or diplomatic relations. The change cannot fail, however, to have an effect on Britain's defence industry, which is an important factor in the economy and one of its more successful sectors and in which any serious disturbance would be less than welcome.

Among many misapprehensions about neutrality is the idea that it entails the acceptance of some rigid ideological code of conduct on the subject of arms manufacture and sales. This is quite untrue. Neutral countries are considerable manufacturers of arms and increasingly sell them abroad, although some, at least, of them regulate their sales and choose their customers in a somewhat more circumspect manner than the more aggressive salesmen among the countries of NATO and the Warsaw Pact. The idea persists, however, and is a potent reason why neutrality is regarded with some suspicion by employers, trade unionists and politicians alike, fearing a threat to profits and employment in a large industry and to a significant volume of valuable export sales. They need not worry. A British move to military non-alignment would treat the subject of arms manufacture and sales in a completely pragmatic and practical way. There would be no reason for any immediate initiative for change.

Soviet methods of espionage and of pirating technology are notorious and efficient. They would consitute just as much of a problem to a militarily non-aligned Britain as they do to her as a member of NATO. She would be very concerned indeed not to embarrass her late allies and not to give comfort or help to those they consider their enemies. She would therefore probably operate controls and impose restrictions on sales abroad of high technology equipment similar to those now, rather uncomfortably, operated by the United States and its allies. In considering sales which might be sensitive in this context, it might be suitable, for a time at least, to agree to consultation before release of substantial items. It would be politic and proper that goodwill and flexibility should take preference over commercial advantage in some such areas.

Although Britain is a substantial armaments exporter, she is a poor fourth in the field to the United States, the USSR and France and she is already much less inclined than any of those three to use arms sales for any political or power-seeking purpose. A change of policy or sentiment in the field would be slow to develop.

The scale and complication of sophisticated weapons make it impossible for any country except a super-power to be self-sufficient in all arms, and Britain is no exception. Nevertheless she has a wide spread of manufactures and does a considerable amount of important research and development work. The Ministry of Defence, independent companies and the universities undertook between them in 1982-3 no less than £1,841 m. of such work. Some projects in this field could probably be slimmed down or discontinued with a new defence policy, but, once again, precipitate action would be a mistake until it was certain that the work being done was clearly superfluous to our requirements in neutrality.

Complications would undoubtedly arise in connexion with the considerable volume of co-operative development and manufacturing ventures which are undertaken in partnership with NATO countries and France, but again there would be no call for any immediate or urgent steps to be taken. In particular, the projects in company with France, which prides herself on an independence which often proves an embarrassment to her partners, would be unlikely to be affected. There seems to be no objection in principle to a neutral country taking part in such schemes. Sweden is on record as having considered the possibility, although the complications which might arise in time of war would obviously require very careful consideration. None of this presents any insuperable barrier to a successful switch to a non-aligned orientation.

This chapter has not tried to present a comprehensive blueprint for the defence of neutral Britain. It has not, for instance, touched on the imaginative and practical scheme for a volunteer auxiliary defence force sponsored by Admiral Hill-Norton and distinguished officers from the other services which was mentioned on p. 56. This could certainly play an important and economical part in a neutral defence structure. The undoubted need for further strengthening of anti-aircraft defence has not been stressed, nor the need for proper civil defence measures. These latter, as in other neutral countries, could offer some protection against fall-out from nuclear warfare elsewhere and would be less controversial, if more expensive, in neutrality since local authorities would not object to them on ideological grounds.

If what has been set out above has indicated that the task of defending our country as a neutral is, given resolve and energy, well within our resources and the present budget, it will have served its purpose.

A change of orientation by Britain will not have the traumatic effects in the international world that it would have produced early in this century, when British policy was a prime factor in the calculations of all the more active nations. Britain is, however, still a substantial power of medium rank and the change-over will inevitably have repercussions beyond our shores. In the next chapter, therefore, we turn to a discussion of some of the effects and reactions which can be expected and try to see whether they should affect our decision.

10. *British Neutrality and the World*

The adoption by Britain of the orientation of military non-alignment will affect a number of states and groupings of states. Since the change is one mainly, but not entirely, of military significance, the countries most affected will naturally be those with whom we have at present a close relationship or interest in the sphere of defensive and military arrangements. Those countries are, first and foremost the United States and the Western Alliance countries with whom we are now allied. The European Community, although not as yet formally concerned with defence, has been showing signs of wanting a say, and France is pressing for a more powerful, and presumably French-inspired, voice in the Alliance through the now moribund Western European Union. Interest in Britain's action can also be expected in the Soviet Union, the other members of the Warsaw Pact, the European neutrals, the Commonwealth and the Third World. Likely reaction in all these quarters needs consideration before the step is taken.

The relationship with NATO is the fundamental basis of Britain's present stance, and the figures in the table show how Britain's defence expenditure compares with the other allies. It would be wrong to read too much into these figures, but they do seem to indicate two rather striking facts. The first is that Britain is bearing more than her fair share of the defence of the European mainland (and getting less defence of her island for her money), and the second that, judging from the figures for population and GDP, it is a gross exaggeration to say, as is often heard, that Britain's support is essential to the viability of NATO. If the mainland countries had to take over the British contribution, they would still have to pay on average only two-thirds of the amount paid by the British now per head and three-quarters of the amount in proportion to GDP.

Defence Expenditures of NATO Countries

	Population (millions)	GDP ($ bn.)	Defence Expenditure ($ bn.)
Belgium	10	84	1.9
Denmark	5	56	1.3
France	54	537	17.9
West Germany	61	659	18.9
Greece	10	38	1.8
Italy	57	347	7.3
Netherlands	14	137	4.5
Norway	4	56	1.7
Portugal	10	23	.6
Spain	38	177	4.5
Turkey	47	52	2.2
Total Mainland Countries	310	2166	62.6
United Kingdom	56	473	25.2
United States	234	3012	239

All figures from *The Military Balance 1983-4*
(International Institute of Strategic Studies)

A great deal of effort has been, and is still being, expended on selling the idea that the military participation of Britain is required for the protection of the continental mainland of Europe. This was true at the time of the formation of the Alliance, when France and Germany, for different reasons, had not recovered sufficiently from their defeats to take an adequate part in their own defence. Now West Germany is rebuilt and France is clear of those colonial commitments which sapped her growing strength after the liberation of Europe. Each of these two states is now stronger and more vigorous than Britain, and the recovery of the smaller NATO members who were overcome in the 1939 war is also complete.

Britain's contribution to the defence of these nations is, unlike the contribution of the United States, at the expense of her own security and in no way contributes to it. To defend Europe in Europe keeps war away from the United States. To defend Europe in Europe brings war closer to the United Kingdom. Britain contains less than one-sixth of the population of the European members of the Western Alliance and just over one-sixth of its productive capacity. Pushing Britain to the very forefront of the confrontation with the Soviet bloc is good business for everyone except us. The countries of the mainland are quite strong enough to preserve the shape of their present defence strategy, if that is what they wish, without help from Britain. It is not our business to tell these nations how to arrange their affairs, but to pretend that they have an absolute need for Britain to defend them is nonsense.

A last argument for the supposedly 'vital' importance of Britain in NATO is that she is the main base and channel for reinforcement from across the Atlantic. This is no more than a military myth. The reality is that because of her small size, open position and lack of defences, a more circuitous but less vulnerable route from America to Europe than that through Britain would make the very doubtful concept of reinforcement more credible. In a real emergency it is a fair guess that it would be adopted anyway. If there are to be US reinforcements taking part in the 'next' war in Europe, there won't be time for them to come to England, drink the whisky and kiss the girls before re-embarking for the continent.

Whatever shape a war between the Soviet Union and the United States might take, it isn't going to be like that. To think it will be is 'fighting the last war' with a vengeance.

Although the circumstances are now completely different from those which obtained when Britain helped to form the Alliance, and the Alliance has the resources, if it has the will, to remain viable after Britain's departure, we must ask whether the members would be likely, as is sometimes suggested, to disband on receiving notice that Britain wished to withdraw.

No one could expect that the mainland European countries would be pleased that the United Kingdom had decided to withdraw its commitment to their support. It has for thirty-five years made a substantial and free contribution to their defence budgets and their economies, but it was hardly likely to do so for ever. If they see that Britain is determined and able to defend its own shores, airspace and waters against any threats it perceives to itself, and that they are not asked for any contribution to that defence, they will the better solve their own political and military problems, which the table on p. 112 suggests they are well able to do. The rational conclusion is that, provided the United States retains her interest in the continent, the mainland countries are unlikely to decide that the withdrawal of Britain is more than an inconvenience, and one which they could well have foreseen.

This leads to the question whether the United States would retain her interest in Europe if Britain left her Alliance. Is it possible that British defection, for that is how it will be seen, would finally undermine American confidence in Europe? Would the American public begin to say: 'First the Frogs chucked us out, now the goddam Limeys give us the push, next it'll be the Krauts. If they don't want us to defend them, let's get the hell out of it and see how they like it under the Commies.' Could the United States emulate the events of 1919 and, at the behest of an isolationist and anti-European Congress, retire from the international scene? Would the loss of the British fleet and the British forces in Germany tip the scale?

It is very unlikely. The America of the 1980s is quite unlike the America of 1919. The tide of events from 1941, and probably from much earlier, has driven America inexorably into world leadership, world involvement, world competition, world rivalry. American investment, trade, ownership and finance have brought responsibilities which cannot be shrugged off. They are on a scale and of a kind quite different from 1919, making it impossible for the United States to leave the stage as she did then.

Europe is now the chief among a number of American interests which the United States cannot and will not abandon. Although the British decision to leave the Alliance will be a blow to American pride and a nuisance for American organisation, it will not fundamentally alter the facts of international life as seen by US policy makers. The counter-blow to British pride is that it is already West Germany and not Britain which is the premier US ally, the fulcrum of the Alliance, the partner in Europe who really matters. Germany's dominant position in Central Europe, its great financial and industrial strength, its increasing involvement overseas and its relation with its sister state within the Warsaw Pact – all these factors combine to make the Federal Republic by far the most precious and least expendable American interest in Europe. It is Germany who sustains, just as it is Germany who requires, the American commitment to Europe.

Neutralism is sometimes referred to, chiefly by American politicians, as if it were some kind of disease, with the inference that it may be contagious as well as fatal. It seems unlikely, however, that Britain's move will have much immediate effect on the European members of the Alliance. They have their own preoccupations and politics and, like Britain, their responsibility is to the welfare of their own people as best they see it. Some possible developments can be suggested, but they are imprecise and mostly quite unlikely.

Could Spain and Greece, recently joined and somewhat uncertain members, be influenced to change their minds? Would Italy's political instability worsen? Would France, already outside NATO, draw further away from the Alliance? Would the Benelux countries and Denmark, traditionally close to Britain, follow her into neutrality? Would Norway and Turkey, on the outer flanks, feel more isolated and less secure? Above all, would West Germany herself, no longer quiescent and docile but seething with political, moral and intellectual energy, strike out a line of her own, some new, perhaps anti-American, *Ost Politik*?

It is soon established that there is little substance in any of these suggestions, despite a basis of plausibility in most of them. Taking them in order, Spain is only likely to assess the British move in relation to her position over Gibraltar. She has distanced herself from Britain on this account and would probably be not unwilling to accept closer and possibly profitable links with the United States and NATO on Britain's departure.

Greece has also lost her traditional affiliation with Britain and would be little affected in her policies by our departure. Neither of these countries nor Italy is in the least likely to be tempted by the 'example' of Britain. Their political courses are individual and not much connected with the Britain of today.

France has already shown her independence when, under de Gaulle, she moved unceremoniously out of NATO; since then, she has been furtively edging back towards a closer association. France has never been very comfortable in association with Britain and will probably appreciate the opportunity to assert her leadership in Europe in a way she finds more difficult with Britain at her elbow.

The smaller countries on the Channel and North Sea seaboard cannot fail to be upset by the British move. They have always relied on the British presence as some kind of balance to offset the greater neighbours on their land borders, but, much as Britain values, and will continue to value, their friendship and respect, events over the last years in the EEC have shown that Britain is no longer either an effective or a necessary factor in their new position in Europe or in NATO.

Norway might be the NATO country most affected by British neutrality. The possibility cannot be ruled out that the small population of this relatively large land might have an urge to revert to its tradition of neutrality, although its experience in Hitler's war may have been disastrous enough to make the security offered by NATO seem preferable to taking sole responsibility for her direct border with the Soviet Union and for the Northern harbours which cover the exit routes from Murmansk to the open sea.

Britain has relinquished most of the interest and influence she had in the Eastern Mediterranean, once very important in her policies, and Turkey could view Britain's departure from

NATO with complete equanimity. It is our abiding hope to relinquish our share in the 'residual' problems of Cyprus as soon as that can be effected without abrogating the responsibilities we have accepted and, if possible, without further alienating Greek and Turk in that once happy land.

With Britain as neutral, German influence in the Western Alliance will become more marked, which is bound to cause some disquiet on both sides of the Iron Curtain, where suspicions of German revanchism are never far from the surface. But the reality is that Germany is the richest and most powerful nation in Europe. It is not only right but inevitable that Germany will in future accept the full share of political responsibility which, by very wisely keeping a low profile since her defeat in 1945, she has not so far sought. The great German liberal and intellectual tradition, submerged from Bismarck to Hitler, has reasserted itself since the defeat of 1945. One can hope it will remain in the ascendant. Germany is the key to Central Europe and it is Germans who will ultimately settle the destiny of the area. Britain has neither the power nor the right nor the interest to influence the solutions when they come, which will not be tomorrow.

Nor does German policy concern itself overmuch with Britain except in such matters as EEC squabbling. The Germany of today is willing enough to accept British help with her defence and the two nations are significant trading partners, but the German dilemma since the Adenauer days has been unconnected with Britain: it is whether the United States or France shall be her closest ally. There can be little doubt that, in spite of occasional bouts of anti-Americanism on the fringes of politics, her preference will lie across the Atlantic. Britain took the step, in conjunction with her allies, of trusting the Germans to rearm in 1955. Now that they have reached a position of strength we must accept that they have the right and responsibility of settling their own problems in their own way.

These considerations support the view that the United States and the mainland members of the Western Alliance are unlikely to alter their perceptions of how they stand in Europe as a result of a change in British orientation. It is widely accepted that there is now at least an element of stability in the

situation in Europe, in spite of the immense destructive power
which lurks there. We have to ask whether the departure of
Britain from the Alliance into a posture of armed defensive
neutrality would be a factor tending towards the
'destabilisation' of this state of relative calm.

Destabilisation is an emotive word which has come to
convey the idea that, even in a situation of only comparative
stability, any change will necessarily tend to undermine that
stability. This is manifestly untrue, since there must and will
be changes in the circumstances and policies of members of
the international community. It is singularly defeatist, in a
situation which is obviously far from perfect, to assume that all
change must be for the worse.

The existing moderate degree of stability in Europe subsists
on reciprocal perceptions by the super-powers. Russia
believes that the United States is deterred from stirring up
trouble in the Eastern European satellite countries and from
taking direct action against communism (as directed in the
'Captive Nations' Resolution of Congress) by Soviet military
power. The United States believes that Russia is deterred from
making further military inroads into Western Europe only by
the American guarantee to the countries of the Western
Alliance, the guarantee being underlined by the American
presence among them.

There is no reason to suppose that the admittedly uneasy
stability engendered by these perceptions is going to be
disturbed by the transfer of British military weight from the
defence of Germany to the defence of Britain. If British
military weight were to be substantially reduced, and an
undefended Britain were seen to be edging towards the
communist camp, the possibility, however remote, that
British bases might, through pressure or acquiescence,
become available to the Soviets, would certainly introduce an
element of destabilisation. But there is absolutely no prospect
of such things occurring.

So long, then, as British defence remains substantial and
efficient, the changes to the European situation brought about
by British neutrality are twofold: the American guarantee to
Britain is removed; and the British guarantee to Germany and
the mainland countries is removed. It is difficult to see how
either of these changes specifically tends towards any

'destabilisation' of the European situation. Certainly they will not bring about, of themselves, the collapse or disbandment of the Western Alliance, nor any immediate change in the policies of its members. These will only come about with some radical change either in the world or in their perceptions of it.

It is totally unlikely that the United States will feel that if she is denied the direct support of British power she will not wish, or will not be able, to maintain her military position in Europe. Her stance may change somewhat, particularly in the naval sense. She could abandon, probably with relief, the hazardous Northern reinforcement route to which she is now committed, and which must be a perpetual worry in her planning. Longer but safer routes will be found to the South, much further from Russian bases. It will not be the absence of Britain from her Alliance which will trigger off the quiescent American urge to 'bring the boys home'. The day will come, but its advent will be slow and carefully planned. The United States, must, one day, pull out of Western Europe, just as, one day, the Soviets will pull out of Eastern Europe. For both the super-powers this is, ultimately, only common sense. But there is no chance, or for that matter desirability, that this happy outcome will transpire without long and complex negotiations during which both sides will ask for, and eventually receive and give, assurances which will leave Europe as well as the two super-powers with reasonable security. What shape these negotiations and assurances will take cannot now be foreseen any more than can the circumstances in which even discussions towards starting negotiations could begin. But if British neutrality brings the possibility nearer, even by a few years, it will have done the world a great service.

The United States and the European NATO countries are amongst Britain's most important trading partners. Our markets in commodities, investment and currencies and our arrangements in banking, insurance, communications and international co-operation are very closely meshed. We come of similar or allied cultural traditions and roots. So much mutual interest breeds obligations as well as advantages and there are those who say that military obligations are, and should be, included. We have to ask whether a refusal by Britain to take any further military part in the Western Alliance will destroy or affect these long-standing and valued relationships and whether it might undermine the complex web of personal and business contacts and arrangements which are the essence of our dealings with these countries. Could they, and would they, on either an official or unofficial level, operate any wounding sanctions against us to punish us for our change of course?

What in particular of the once vaunted 'special relationship' with the United States, and what of our rather shaky participation in the EEC? Britain has lived by trade and, after North Sea oil, will have to do so again. Shall we, by taking this step in our defence arrangements, be doing ourselves irreparable damage by wounding our closest associates?

The truth about the so-called 'special relationship' with the United States is that it hasn't been particularly special for quite some time. It was conjured up in the minds of British publicists as a substitute for the vanished status of equality between the two countries, but American politicians have never welcomed or even admitted the concept. President Roosevelt's personal 'special relation' with Prime Minister Churchill was real and useful to both countries in the specific circumstances of the war, but it did not affect the President's dislike of the British Empire nor his desire for its dissolution. The great generosity of the Marshall Plan was tendered to all Europe and in no way specially for Britain. The relationship between the United States and the United Kingdom, although lubricated by the common language, is now no more special than that which the US, with its wide international interests, has with many other countries.

The Western world, composed of free and independent states, many of them democracies, would be denying its most cherished principles if, by some form of governmental ostracism, it tried to force a nation whose devotion to those principles is not in question into the continuance of a policy which it no longer regarded as being in its interests.

A temporary cooling of diplomatic relations, a less intimate relationship with the present allies following the withdrawal of contacts and co-operation in the military and intelligence fields, would be likely. But this is a price Britain could willingly pay and which would anyway be necessary to the building of her new place in the world. An independent neutral would not have, and would not wish to have, a standing in international affairs similar to that of an ally and satellite in one of the great alliances. You leave one club and join another. The old one may have seemed glamorous, giving admission to gatherings self-styled as important, but the new one can in time be just as effective, useful and rewarding.

Governmental pressures to exert formal or informal sanctions against a newly neutral Britain would probably in practice be less important than reactions on the personal plane. British foreign contacts and connexions have been built up over many years of international trading, travel, finance and culture. They are wider and more comprehensive than those of any comparable nation. Will the basis of this network, which is respect for Britain and for her traditions and methods, be partially or totally eroded by the cessation of British military support for the American Alliance in confrontation with Soviet Russia?

This is of great importance. If individuals in the Western Alliance, American and European, see British withdrawal simply as taking what is sometimes called 'a free ride', sheltering under the United States' nuclear umbrella and accepting, without payment, defence by America and its allies against a predatory Soviet Union, much harmful resentment against Britain could be engendered. It has to be accepted that, in circles irrevocably committed to the ultra-hawkish view, this attitude will persist, inaccurate as it is.

An equally damaging misrepresentation is that British withdrawal from the military confrontation means withdrawal of opposition to the seamy side of the communist ideology, its tyranny and denial of human rights in flagrant contravention of the United Nations Charter. These suggestions need the most vigorous contradiction. Neutral Britain would remain committed to the highest ideals in these matters and, as in the cases of Sweden and Switzerland, independence would add significance to her views.

To counter such innuendos effectively it is necessary that the principles underlying British neutrality be proclaimed with the utmost frequency, clarity and simplicity. Since these principles are the essence of the relationship of neutral Britain with the world, it may be opportune to restate them in this chapter. They are:

(1) That Britain is not conscious of any military threat to her independence and integrity which she cannot deal with herself;

(2) That Britain does not require the protection of American or Soviet nuclear arsenals, and would in no circumstances countenance their use or threatened use in her defence;

(3) That Britain's engagement to assist in the defence of mainland Europe, made thirty-five years ago, is no longer necessary in the changed circumstances of Europe today;

(4) That Britain, having relinquished the status of a world power, has no desire for expansion or military adventure and does not believe that any power has demands on her which cannot be settled by negotiation. Accordingly Britain proposes in future to maintain only such military establishment as she considers necessary for the defence of the United Kingdom and such residual Commonwealth responsibilities as remain to her;

(5) That Britain's commitments to the principles of the United Nations Charter are unchanged;

(6) That Britain believes that her contributions to the causes of freedom and democracy are best made on a political and not on a military plane;

(7) That Britain's action is taken in view of the particular circumstances, geographical, political, military and industrial, which apply to the United Kingdom. Britain will continue to respect the policies of nations whose circumstances and perceptions are different from hers; and

(8) That Britain appreciates that each of the super-powers, and their allies, may feel threatened ideologically and militarily by the members of the opposing bloc. Britain does not feel so threatened, and believes that her contribution to world stability is best made outside the super-power confrontation.

By continued and forceful expression of these principles, Britain and the British people will be able to persuade their friends and contacts throughout the world that British withdrawal, for the first time for three hundred years, from the military centre of the international stage is a right and reasonable acceptance of what is historically inevitable.

It would be idle to pretend that no friends will be lost and no relationships disturbed. But these wounds will heal surprisingly soon. Rearrangements of national attitudes following great disturbances are a part of history. There have been no greater disturbances in history than those of the last fifty years and it would be absurd to expect that all the rearrangements made necessary by those disturbances have yet been completed.

Britain need not fear too much from the concentration of minds and new policies which will inevitably be brought about within the Western Alliance by her action. It will not be too long thereafter that she will begin to receive from around the world appreciable rewards, which will come to her through the reliability, stability and fixity of purpose which are attributes very generally associated with nations adopting the stance of neutrality.

Looking across the Iron Curtain, can we see any likelihood of substantial reactions or changes of policy or outlook within the Warsaw Pact as a result of British withdrawal from NATO? Will the balance of power be disturbed? Will the Soviets see the move as the first sign of the disintegration of their sworn opponents? Will Moscow step up its pressures in Europe and elsewhere? Will the ring of restive satellites in Eastern Europe find any message for themselves? Will the world temperature rise or fall? Will the arms race slow down? Will Russian paranoia about encirclement decrease?

The answers to most of these questions can only be highly speculative, but it can be taken as sure that immediate and visible results of British neutrality will be neither rapid nor spectacular. Moscow will regard the change with its customary caution, even suspicion, while making some propaganda capital out of it. It is most unlikely that there will be any substantial change in the confrontation tactics of the Kremlin, nor will Britain's withdrawal from the arms race much affect either of the principal runners. The very lack of visible effect will emphasise to the world that the confrontation really is between the super-powers themselves and that the basis of it is little influenced by any factor outside the control of one or other of them.

Significant to ourselves, and not without interest to the rest of the world, will be the attitude taken up by the Soviet Union towards a newly neutral Britain. Will she try to woo us into her orbit, pressurise us into her ways, or simply ignore the change?

It seems likely that the immediate visible reaction will be very mild, underlining the fact that, except for the special case of Finland, close neighbour and ex-Imperial-Russian territory, for Moscow there is little to choose between a neutral capitalist country and an Alliance capitalist country. Britain should be neither surprised nor chagrined. It is to be hoped that she will have made very clear at the time of leaving the Alliance that she has no intention of being drawn any closer to the Russian orbit through her action. She will be wise to pre-empt any developments by reducing her diplomatic representation in Moscow and requesting a parallel reduction in the Soviet Embassy and spy network here. To begin with we should set the Soviets a strict example of correct but discreetly distant relations.

Possibly the most interesting study will be of the psychological effects in the Soviet satellites. No one should expect any of these countries to take any open steps to change their relations with the Soviets following the British action. Any precipitate moves would react to their disadvantage, but they will watch developments with great interest and it can hardly fail to conjure up long-term dreams of one day breaking the log jam in which they are held.

At the mention of British neutrality the first objection usually heard is the 'argument from duress'. This suggests that Britain is so completely in thrall to the American Alliance and is so enmeshed in NATO that there is no practical way to loosen the bonds. In this view we have gone so far and given so much that we have effectively lost our freedom of action. We are tied to the defence of Germany and military confrontation with Russia for as long as America and her allies say we shall be.

The coils of involvement certainly wind more tightly around us every year. Our best forces are far from home and under the command of an American general. We supply political, military and civilian staff to all the committees, headquarters and formations of NATO, which stretch from Virginia to

Frankfurt and from Norway to the Mediterranean. We are becoming involved farther afield. Alliance secrets are in our files and much of our equipment and arms come from America or West European sources. Joint manufacturing ventures were mentioned in the last chapter and there is much joint design, planning and liaison at all levels. Finance, commerce, politics, administration and staff work are closely co-ordinated. Probably never, in peace or war, has a multinational organisation of such scope and complexity been devised. The difficulties of disentanglement should not be underestimated or ignored, but neither must they be exaggerated.

In our withdrawal from the Alliance there will be snags and difficulties galore and we should certainly take every care to give all help and co-operation possible to smooth the task for our erstwhile allies. We should try to arrange the timetables for British withdrawal from the Continent, and NATO and American withdrawal from Britain, in the way least painful to, and with the maximum of consideration for, the other nations involved. The argument that 'it can't be done' will find echoes in Britain, not least from the many people who have a vested interest in the *status quo*. It will be used with effect by the French, who will resent the threat to their conveniently equivocal position in the Alliance, and by the Germans, who will complain at the greater expense they may have to undertake in their own defence. The Americans will be little less vociferous, but many greater and more difficult operations have been undertaken and this one can and will be achieved if Britain insists that it is her destiny.

The timescale will be of great importance and here again Britain should show as much flexibility as possible. When France withdrew from NATO, the whole operation, which included moving the main headquarters of the organisation, was complete within the statutory one year's notice given. Britain should act with more cicumspection and allow longer, but without allowing the momentum of change to flag. A final deadline of three years with a target of two might be reasonable.

The argument from duress, that Britain has no practical alternative to her place in the American Alliance, is mostly based on vested interests, distaste for change, laziness, lack of enterprise and initiative, fear of the unknown. If neutrality, closely examined, is the right orientation for Britain, it can be won. We must think of the rewards, not of the difficulties which, as Churchill was wont to say, will speak for themselves.

In examining the option of military non-alignment, the concern so far has, quite naturally, been mostly with negatives, the commitments we should discard and the dangers we should avoid. These aspects are the most important in the immediate task of coming to a decision, but we should not, on that account, be deceived into thinking of neutrality as a negative stance, a withdrawal from the international arena, an opting out from the great affairs of the world.

Nothing could be further from the truth. The international activities of all the five prominent European neutrals are vigorous and effective. Sweden is the acknowledged world centre of 'peace' studies and activities, Switzerland the home and founder of the Red Cross, Yugoslavia is a respected leader of the Third World states, Austria and Finland are centres for East/West contacts. All are regular and generous givers of moral and military support for United Nations peacekeeping activities and are favourite venues for conferences and meetings where an atmosphere of calm and impartiality can be of substantial help to the participants.

Neutral Britain would naturally not be over-active in international affairs until she had come to terms with her new orientation and had been generally accepted in it. Soon, however, she would again play a full part at the United Nations and in the diplomatic world. The possibility is far from negligible that the strength and authority she would bring to the non-aligned sector would make it a much more positive force in the not too distant future.

The East-West divide often seems the world's most urgent and difficult problem, but it is likely that what has come to be called the North/South breach, the gap between the rich and poor countries, may ultimately present a more potent threat to world stability and security. In this sphere the neutrals have already played a conspicuous part and, probably more than other nations, they have gained the confidence and respect of the less developed countries. With the addition of such a power as Britain, which has access to the innermost financial sanctums and a veto in the Security Council, the neutralist influence might bring the forums which grapple with these problems towards a more co-operative and less abrasive approach to the dangers which are so widely perceived.

It is too much to hope that neutral opinion will soon or seriously affect the arms race or the confrontation between the super-powers, but even the smallest addition to tranquillity and stability is some help to a troubled world in which a high proportion of the population fervently wish to remain outside that confrontation.

It would be premature to expect too much too soon, but Britain's role in world affairs, quiescent at present, may in neutrality blossom and increase.

11. *British Neutrality and the British*

In a democracy unanimity is rare. The national commitment to neutrality in Sweden, Switzerland and Austria does, however, come very close to being unanimous. For Britain this is too much to hope for immediately, but the necessary conditions for neutrality do include a considerable degree of consensus. This applies to the public in general, but there is also a need for willing acceptance of the idea by those concerned with decision making. Consensus need not extend beyond this one subject and in no way inhibits wide differences on many other aspects of policy.

The starting point of consensus is that all realise and accept that Britain is now a lesser power with only minor capacity to influence international affairs.

From this stem three main points: that there is no reason or profit in involving ourselves in the political instability and attendant dangers in Eastern Europe; that we have no direct contribution to make to the solution of the German problem; and that we should distance ourselves from the openly hostile attitudes of the super-powers to one another, attitudes through which they may, accidentally, deliberately or uncontrollably, involve themselves and their allies in a disaster of incredible magnitude.

Prince Metternich of Austria, commenting on his own downfall as the archpriest of outworn regimes, said when he left Vienna: 'It is useless to close the gates against ideas. They overleap them.' So far the idea of neutrality for the new Britain has lacked the ventilation and discussion necessary to give it strength. More especially, discussion is needed without sidetracking or diversions implying a connexion between neutrality and such notions as pacifism, disarmament or appeasement. Such schemes and dreams only confuse and impede consideration of the simple, hard-headed and practical proposal of a Britain committed to neutrality in war and military non-alignment in peace, responsible for its own defence in freedom and independence.

When this idea is ready to overleap the gates which at present contain it, the change in orientation will still need a political decision which has to be taken by political means and in the political arena. No political party has as yet adopted neutrality as a fundamental part of its policy.

In one sense this may for a time be no bad thing. The divisions and antipathies between the main parties in Britain are so deep that if any one of them were formally to espouse the cause of British neutrality, that would be enough to ensure that all ears in all other parties were firmly shut even to discussion of the proposal.

It is tempting, therefore, to suggest that a matter of such importance should ultimately be settled by referendum, this being the only way that the whole electorate can be consulted and pronounce on a single issue. There would, however, have to be a period of very intense and powerful lobbying before party leaders would permit recourse to the device which is, in any case, viewed with some suspicion in an England accustomed for many centuries to accept the decisions of its Parliament. A consensus in Parliament, reflecting the general approval of the country, would be much preferable, although the inertia of establishment views and the influence of vested interests will not be easy to dislodge within the party machines. So in the first place neutrality must seek to cross party lines and appeal to the personal judgement and common sense of electors of every shade of political opinion. The aim must be to promote open discussion of the complex issues involved, trying to surmount the opposition of prejudice, vested interest and habit. Only calm and reasoned appraisal of the costs and benefits of the policy to Britain and the world will bring the right decision.

Neutrality is essentially to do with the subject of peace. Nations which have no likely reason or intention of going to war assume the stance of neutrality as being the orientation most likely to protect their citizens from the danger of war. Thereby they make a contribution to international stability and peace. The adoption of neutrality is essentially a statement of peaceful intentions, a formal Declaration of Peace.

The lack of informed discussion about neutrality which has been noted above is not due to any lack of discussion about peace, which is continuous and active. This being so, we have to ask whether there is any relationship, either of affiliation or antagonism, between the orientation of military non-alignment which has been put forward here, and what has become known as the 'Peace Movement'. This is spearheaded in Britain by the vociferous and energetic Campaign for Nuclear Disarmament (CND).

The aims of CND, as set out in the organisation's constitutional document, are commendably simple. They are set out in two sentences but may conveniently be divided into four parts. The primary aim is stated as:

(1) '. . . the unilateral abandonment by Britain of nuclear weapons, nuclear bases and nuclear alliances . . .'
This is a 'pre-requisite for'
(2) '. . . a British foreign policy which has the worldwide abolition of nuclear, chemical and biological weapons leading to general and complete disarmament as its prime objective.'
Then follows opposition to:
(3) 'the manufacture, stockpiling, testing, use and threatened use of nuclear, chemical and biological weapons by any country . . .'
and lastly opposition to:
(4) '. . . the policies of any country or group of countries which make nuclear war more likely, or which hinder progress towards a world without weapons of mass destruction.'

None of these aims directly conflicts with the principles of British neutrality which have been put forward here, but there are fundamental differences in outlook, method and priorities.

In the first chapter were set out the three categories into which a nation's foreign policy aims are divided. These are, first, the 'core' aims, such as security, which are basic and essential. Then come the lesser aims which can be achieved by routine transactions. Last are those 'far-reaching hopes' towards which a nation can work in the international sphere, but which are in practice beyond the capacity of any but the super-powers to bring to fruition.

However much we may regret it, neither the 'prime objective' prescribed for Britain's foreign policy in CND's second aim, nor the 'opposition' voiced in the third and fourth, can realistically come into any but the third category of foreign-policy aims for a lesser power. They cannot and should not displace national security as Britain's main 'core' aim.

It may seem surprising, therefore, that CND does not concentrate its activities on the achievement of the first section of its stated aims. Withdrawal from NATO has, however, been specifically ruled out as a main priority aim at successive AGM's. This in spite of the statement in CND's *30 Questions and Answers* document that CND 'works for the dissolution of both (the major military blocs)' and is 'therefore opposed to NATO and aims at a British withdrawal'.

The equivocation is understandable, because CND is faced with a difficult choice by the wording of its constitution. On the one hand, it is to work for the unilateral abandonment by Britain of its nuclear weapons, bases and allies (aim 1); on the other, it wishes to continue to try to exert direct influence on America, the Western allies, the Eastern bloc and the rest of the world (aims 2, 3 and 4).

If Britain decided to adopt neutrality aim 1 could be achieved at a stroke, provided it was approved as national defence policy. By the same stroke, however, it must be admitted that CND would lose most of its ability to pursue its aims 2, 3 and 4. Britain, in concert with other neutrals, could be expected to exert every effort within its limited power to further these aims, but they could not be 'primary' nor could any immediate or direct results be expected. And with Britain outside the Alliance, and Greenham Common an RAF (non-nuclear) base, CND would be a horse without a course, its occupation gone.

A large organisation dealing in controversial matters across a wide spectrum is prone to vagueness in policy statements in order not to lose the support of members with differing viewpoints. The leadership of CND probably has at least two good reasons for playing down that section of its primary aim which calls for the 'abandonment of nuclear alliances'. The first may be that it wishes to retain the support of those who hope that the Western Alliance, including the United States and France, will unilaterally renounce nuclear weapons but remain an Alliance, retaining the British commitment to the continental defence of West Germany. Secondly, it is perhaps not particularly anxious to face up to the implications of well-armed neutrality, which would be the only rational policy after leaving NATO.

Maybe CND will come to see that, as well as being safer without nuclear weapons, Britain would also be safer outside the complications of super-power relations and Eastern European squabbles. At least it can be hoped that members will look seriously at the option of neutrality, and not be blinkered by their obsession that 'peace' is about nothing but nuclear weapons.

Neutrality, like all political concepts, is about people, so at the end of our examination of the policy it is right to ask how the change of orientation will affect the ordinary British citizen. Will any impact be felt outside the corridors of Whitehall and Westminster?

We can only judge from the experiences of other European neutrals, which do seem to give some grounds for hope, since, as we have seen, all their neutralist stances have a strong moral and psychological base. This applies to Sweden, Switzerland and Austria, whose diplomatic, social, trade and ideological ties are overwhelmingly with the free Western world, and also to Yugoslavia, running a communist system in genuine independence.

No one can say for certain that the British people will have similar feelings or reap similar advantages from neutrality. Time will be needed for the change to be assimilated and fully accepted by the individual and to become, as it is in the other neutral countries, a significant part of the normal day-to-day scene.

In the last years of Britain's descent from power, the outward signs such as the disbanding of empire, the decline of industry, the loss of independence and leadership in foreign affairs, have been accompanied by a certain failure of spirit and confidence. The sense of purpose which had been an organic part of life in Britain has drooped and wilted.

Having been thrust into the role of satellite to the United States, even if it is dignified by the title of junior partner in an alliance, has not been a comfortable role for a country long accustomed to independence and leadership. Britain's position in Europe, now less significant than those of West Germany and France, each of whom were humiliated and defeated in a war in which Britain was unconquered and victorious, has been equally unpalatable.

It would be unrealistic to talk about neutrality resuscitating the spirit of Dunkirk or the Battle of Britain or even the Falkland Islands. That wouldn't even be a good thing, since some upsurges cannot by their nature be permanent. Nobody wants a nation of neutralist jingoists.

Nevertheless the fact that we were solely responsible for our own defence, relying on no allies but fighting for no foreigner, resolved to keep the peace for ourselves and spread it where we can, would be here, as elsewhere, a unifying influence. It would be a tonic to feel that we were free to face the world in our own way, using our own standards, the prestige of neutrality backed by our own history and traditions.

Our democracy might thus find a new, wider base in which the independence, and above all the moderation, of neutrality would penetrate deep into the national consciousness.

British neutrality need be in no way negative. With confidence and unity regained by relinquishing our place in the dangerous East/West conflict, we could take more initiative and responsibility in the equally difficult and even more important North/South encounter. Britain would soon find herself playing a worthy and independent part in the world scene – and a far more interesting one than chugging along towards Armageddon.

Here, maybe, is the true answer to the American Secretary of State who said that Britain had lost an Empire but failed to find a role. The true role which Britain has been seeking is a return to independence in the orientation of military non-alignment, commonly called Neutrality.